1981

ADVANCES IN LIFELONG E[...]

CURRICULUM INTEGRATION
AND
LIFELONG EDUCATION

A Contribution to the Improvement of
School Curricula

CURRICULUM INTEGRATION AND
AND
LIFELONG EDUCATION

A Contribution to the Improvement of
School Curricula

by

JAMES B. INGRAM

UNESCO DIVISION OF STRUCTURES, CONTENTS AND METHODS
OF EDUCATION, PARIS
UNESCO INSTITUTE FOR EDUCATION, HAMBURG
and
PERGAMON PRESS
OXFORD · NEW YORK · TORONTO · SYDNEY · PARIS · FRANKFURT

U.K.	Pergamon Press Ltd., Headington Hill Hall, Oxford OX3 0BW, England
U.S.A.	Pergamon Press Inc., Maxwell House, Fairview Park, Elmsford, New York 10523, U.S.A.
CANADA	Pergamon of Canada, Suite 104, 150 Consumers Road, Willowdale, Ontario M2 J1P9, Canada
AUSTRALIA	Pergamon Press (Aust.) Pty. Ltd., P.O. Box 544, Potts Point, N.S.W. 2011, Australia
FRANCE	Pergamon Press SARL, 24 rue des Ecoles, 75240 Paris, Cedex 05, France
FEDERAL REPUBLIC OF GERMANY	Pergamon Press GmbH, 6242 Kronberg-Taunus, Pferdstrasse 1, Federal Republic of Germany

First edition 1979

British Library Cataloguing in Publication Data

Ingram, James B
Curriculum integration and lifelong education.
(Advances in lifelong education; vol.6).
1. Continuing education - Curricula
I. Title II. Unesco. Institute for Education
III. Series
374   LC5225.C/   78-41155

ISBN 0-08-024301-0   Hardcover (Pergamon)
ISBN 0-08-024300-2   Flexicover (Pergamon)
ISBN 92-820-1018-x   Hardcover (UIE)
ISBN 92-820-1019-8   Flexicover (UIE)

In order to make this volume available as economically and as rapidly as possible the author's typescript has been reproduced in its original form. This method unfortunately has its typographical limitations but it is hoped that they in no way distract the reader.

Printed and bound at William Clowes & Sons Limited, Beccles and London

ABOUT THE AUTHOR

INGRAM, J. B. (United Kingdom). Graduate in Arts, Divinity and Education of the Universities of Aberdeen and Edinburgh. After a period of school teaching in Glasgow he joined the staff of Bulawayo Teachers College in what was then Southern Rhodesia. In 1965 he became a lecturer in education at the University College of Rhodesia and Nyasaland. He returned to Britain in 1970 where he held the post of lecturer at the City of Leeds and Carnegie College of Education and later of principal lecturer in Curriculum Studies at the Margaret McMillan College of Education, Bradford. He is currently director of the B.Ed. Course at Bradford College and has published in the *Journal of Curriculum Studies*.

CONTENTS

Contents

Contents

FOREWORD

Lifelong Education is regarded in the UNESCO programme as a principle which is likely to direct and influence all innovation and/or reform of educational structures, contents and methods as well as teacher training. Education authorities and researchers as well as teachers are paying more and more attention to the application of this principle in the preparation and implementation of educational or curriculum reform. It is proving to be a complex undertaking, yet one can no longer say that Lifelong Education is merely the concept or ideal of certain philosophers. Mr. Ingram's study is the result of a collaboration between the Division of Educational Structures, Contents and Methods of the Secretariat and the Unesco Institute for Education. It is one of the several studies conducted by UNESCO as a contribution to the improvement of school curricula. Among them may be mentioned:

- evaluation of curriculum content in relation to the requirements of the working world, educational counselling and vocational guidance;

- school curriculum as one of the early phases of Lifelong Learning;

- achievements in the development of methodologies for curriculum work in the perspective of Lifelong Education.

One of the most frequent requirements mentioned in the literature on Lifelong Education is the co-ordination of the various elements influencing individual learning. Such co-ordination may follow different patterns, depending on the nature of the factors concerned. As a result different terms are used to refer to it, such as "articulation", "integration", "co-operation", "complementation", "equivalence", etc.

Despite the importance attached to co-ordination, it is not considered an end in itself. It is only a means to facilitate the individual's intentional learning throughout his or

xiii

her life. It applies primarily to the services established to
support such learning, but it may also include specific references to learning opportunities and influences of a spontaneous
nature.

Such a requirement is not new in education. Long-accept-
ed educational principles demand, for instance, that school and
family "co-operate", that the successive grades and levels of
an educational system are "articulated" with each other, that
educational services provided by different Ministries are "coordinated", that the various subjects or learning areas of the
curriculum are "integrated", that the parallel streams of secondary education have "equivalent" value, etc.

The justification for such a requirement which is not exclusive to education, but also occurs in other sectors (cultural
integration, social integration, economic integration, etc.)
originates from three sources. Logical consistency requires
that all influences affecting *one* learning process be articulated or integrated. Principles of operational efficiency and
economic use of resources support the need for operational co-
ordination among the intervening factors in this process.
Finally, the need for harmony is the reason for requiring that
all factors be considered as building up a well-balanced whole.

Lifelong Education does not provide any new evidence jus-
tifying articulation of the factors affecting individual learning. It only adds new dimensions and consequently new modalities of articulation. One of the added dimensions is that of
time. Planned learning is no longer concentrated within the
phases of childhood, adolescence and youth. It has to continue
during adult life, though under different circumstances. Traditionally, articulation and co-ordination were required among
the educational opportunities and influences affecting the
learning process at early ages. In the perspective of Lifelong
Education such a requirement is applicable to educational factors with impact on the learning process during the whole life,
and particularly to those factors affecting adult learning.

A further dimension concerns the number of factors to
which a large variety of modalities of co-ordination is to be
applied. Traditionally, articulation was meant to be *subordination* to the normal school system. As a consequence, the family, for instance, was expected to support the school. Major
educational programmes offered by such Ministries as Agriculture,
Labour, Interior, Defence and Health, were to be subjected to

the standards of the school system. Within the perspective of
Lifelong Education programmes outside of the school system, and
other learning opportunities such as the ones provided by the
place of work, by leisure programmes, etc., have a right of
their own, and a learning value to be assessed in comparison
with their own objectives and criteria. All of them are to be
considered as no less valid a source of learning than the school
system, and as such are to be co-ordinated.

A third dimension added by the perspective of Lifelong
Education relates to the articulation of all factors and influences of learning into an overall network of learning opportunities and services. As a consequence each component of the
network maintains its *specific function* but gains a *relative
role* within the overall network as well as a *sequential value*
derived from the particular stage of the lifelong learning process to which it corresponds. Traditionally, for instance,
compulsory education was conceived as providing merely the
package of knowledge, intellectual skills and attitudes required not to be an illiterate in a specific country. No *sequential value* was attached to it, and its *relative importance*
was ignored. Consequently, compulsory education was conducted
and evaluated as a terminal education of low status. Within
the perspective of Lifelong Education, compulsory schooling is
conceived as an educational phase, providing the basic requirements for lifelong learning.

Despite the relatively frequent reference to articulation,
integration, etc. in educational literature, both in the field
of traditional education and Lifelong Education, the subject
remains a very complex one, with urgent need for research and
study. Sometimes general statements are made, which fail to
recognise that there is no one clear-cut reality behind the
terminology, and that the terminology in fact covers an extensive variety of situations and conditions, very often with
little in common. Such statements have already led to well
deserved criticism of the ethical implications of this idea and
of the feasibility of a concept of Lifelong Education in which
spontaneous learning influences (family, peer groups, radio
programmes, etc.) are to be "*manipulated*" into a global system
of education under the control of the Ministry of Education.

There is an evident need for more analytical, comprehensive, and refined conceptual work leading to the identification
of functions, categories, components, etc. of integration in
the field of education. In addition, there is a need to work

xvi   Curriculum Integration and Lifelong Education

out the practical implications of this conception. Different patterns of implementation under the various categories of integration, their objectives, preconditions, conclusions and implications need to be identified and evaluated. Finally, there is a need for a gradually developed, research validated theory of articulation in education.

Intended primarily for curriculum specialists, educationists and interested researchers, the present study could also be of interest to teachers and educators engaged in the furtherance of Lifelong Education and its institutionalisation.

We would like to express our thanks to Mr. Ingram who has carried out this study with the dedication, scholarship and modesty which characterise his long work in education.

Dr. M. Dino Carelli
Director of the Unesco
Institute for Education
UNESCO, Hamburg

Dr. George Vaideanu
Chief of the Section Structures
and Contents of Education
UNESCO, Paris

INTRODUCTION

1.   The Nature and Purpose of the Study

Lifelong education has in recent years proved to be a fertile field for educational thought and research. Its richness is amply exemplified in the spate of literature and amount of discussion that have been generated since its adoption in 1972 as the focus for the research programme of the Unesco Institute for Education. Yet these developments in themselves barely reveal the considerable effect that the idea has had on educational thought and practice throughout the world. The implications of the idea are being continually mediated through an unfolding process of interpretation and application and it is to this process that this study makes its small but particular contribution.

Due perhaps to the idealism inherent in the concept, the indebtedness of lifelong education to other developments in educational thought and practice, such as the progressive and adult education movements, has not always been fully recognised. As the significance of the concept is assessed in the context of specific educational areas and activities a more objective appraisal of its potential will no doubt emerge. In general terms the purpose of this study is to initiate this process within the field of curriculum integration. A number of writers, for example Dave (1973), have claimed that integration is a focal concept in any consideration of education as a lifelong activity. By reviewing therefore what is known of curriculum integration it is reasonable to expect that the meaning and feasibility of integration within the perspective of lifelong education may gain in clarity and realism. Within the compass of a small study there are clearly limits to such an undertaking and these define its scope and structure.

2.   The Scope and Structure of the Study

The meanings attached to the terms 'curriculum' and 'in-

1

tegration' constitute the first limiting factor. Most defini-
tions of curriculum can be located between the two extremes of
curriculum as content of teaching and curriculum as experience
of learning. In the one case curriculum is a form of the organisation of knowledge, in the other an expression of the learning experience of pupils. This study is necessarily concerned
with both these aspects since the basic issue in curriculum
integration is how to reconcile the obvious diversity of the
one with the apparent unity of the other.

The curriculum to be studied is the school curriculum,
with particular reference to primary and lower secondary schools.
Traditionally, integration has been more characteristic of primary than of secondary education, though its influence in the
secondary sector is spreading. The problems which this is cre-
ating will be examined.

A further constraint is the type and extent of the integration involved. Integration can be both vertical and horizontal. Vertical integration is integration over time and involves the articulation of teaching and learning experiences at
different stages of development. Horizontal integration aims
to harmonise the various dimensions of the curriculum or the
various educational agencies such as home, school and the mass
media. This study concentrates on the horizontal integration
of the curriculum.

The range of literature referred to suffers from two inadequacies. The first is the author's limited linguistic ability, which is largely responsible for most of the literature
being drawn from the English-speaking world, and the second his
selection and arrangement of the material, which to some extent
influenced his choice of authors. It is hoped that neither of
these deficiencies creates too distorted a picture of the contemporary scene in the areas involved.

The extent of the respective contributions of curriculum
integration and lifelong education to each chapter is also influential in determining scope and structure. The focus in the
first chapter is on lifelong education but an attempt is made
to identify the principal characteristics of curriculum integration which are relevant to lifelong education. The chapters
which follow concentrate on curriculum integration and look at
the ways in which it can be achieved, the purposes it can serve,
and the influences it can exert on the classroom and the school.
Aspects that are relevant for lifelong education are noted and

discussed. The 6th chapter presents some of the more pressing
problems of curriculum integration and evaluates its prospects
in the educational enterprise.

The nature of the discussion and the way in which the
material is presented may lead some readers in the earlier chapters to overestimate the value of curriculum integration for
lifelong education. This is partly due to the fact that there
are some very positive points of correspondence between the two
areas and that while these are subject to criticism where appropriate, the more weighty objections to curriculum integration
are reserved for chapter six. It is well that the reader should
therefore keep his expectations in check until these objections
have been considered. He can then, on the basis of the evidence
given, decide for himself how effective a contribution curriculum integration, in one form or another, can make to the furtherance of lifelong education.

CHAPTER 1

LIFELONG EDUCATION AND CURRICULUM INTEGRATION

Though this study is principally concerned with curriculum integration, it views it from the perspective of lifelong education. It is necessary at the outset, therefore, to set the scene by describing this perspective and by identifying in a preliminary form those aspects of curriculum integration which may be important for lifelong education. Such a general survey forms the substance of this chapter. In it a brief account will be given of lifelong education, the nature of the relationship between lifelong education and curriculum integration will be explored, common purposes will be discussed, and possible means of mutual support will be investigated.

1.1   The Relationship between Lifelong Education and
      Curriculum Integration

Lifelong education and curriculum integration have developed as two separate educational notions and practices.

Independent entities are, however, not necessarily debarred from being of benefit to each other. The main point of this study is to find out if lifelong education can be advanced by the use of integrative teaching techniques and if curriculum integration has an ally in lifelong education. At this introductory stage, therefore, a brief account of the distinctive properties of lifelong education and curriculum integration will provide a useful background for what follows.

In the first place it is important to appreciate that while lifelong education is essentially idealistic, curriculum integration has a strong practical orientation. As Cropley (1977) rightly stresses, the notion of lifelong education represents a set of ideals for organising education in ways con-

4

ducive to lifelong learning. Curriculum integration on the
other hand, though by no means lacking ideological support of
one kind or another (Esland, 1971), refers to a variety of educational practices aimed at counteracting the adverse effects
of a fragmented curriculum. At the risk of over-generalisation,
it might be said that the one is a theory in search of practical
application and the other a form of practice in need of theoretical justification.

Other important distinctions follow from this. Lifelong
education is a more global concept than curriculum integration.
The one is general, the other more specific. Lifelong education
encompasses a great variety of educational aspects and a wide
spectrum of practical possibilities, only one of which is curriculum integration. Variations with regard to time are also
significant. Lifelong education embraces the whole of the life-
span; curriculum integration is a problem that arises mainly in
the years of schooling. As an ideal, the one has an eye to the
future, whereas, as a form of practice, the other reflects the
present or recounts the past. One is concerned with what might
be, the other with what has been.

1.2   What is Lifelong Education?

a)   Education and Schooling: A Common Misconception

Many people tend to equate education with schooling and,
in the case of those who take some form of further or higher
education, with life at college or university. Thus in everyday conversation the question is often asked, 'Where were you
educated?' and the answer given, 'At such and such a school or
college'. Even in bookish circles the convention is well en-
trenched, for often bibliographical information, such as on
dust covers or in reference books, contains an entry in the
style, 'Education: Eton and Oxford'.

The implications of this institutional attitude to education are clear. Education is restricted to a particular phase
in life, namely the period of childhood and youth, and identified with specific institutionalised provision for this age
range in schools, colleges and universities. For those children who do not proceed to further or higher education, education and schooling become synonymous.

Confining education in this way has several undesirable

consequences. Though schools are part of society, they nevertheless become in many ways detached from it, and education
which is restricted to the school years tends to become dissociated from life. The value of educational activities that
take place before and after the period of schooling is often
underestimated and the continuity of education as a lifelong
activity seriously affected.

b) Education in Quarantine: The Effects of Isolationism

As social institutions, schools cannot follow an independent line in everything they do. Often they have to support
social processes that are educationally dysfunctional. The
examination system is a case in point. As an instrument of
social engineering rather than a means of educational development, it obstructs the educational opportunities of the many by
ensuring the educational success of the few. Not only does
knowledge become the monopoly of teachers, but certain types of
knowledge become the monopoly of certain types of teacher.
Knowledge is viewed as an object rather than as an aspect of
experience. As a product of the consumer society, it becomes
a form of property to be acquired instead of being an aspect of
experience that is internalised. The principal aim of education becomes, therefore, to increase the quantity of knowledge
rather than improve the quality of life. By emphasising cognitive skills rather than promoting self-realisation, education
as a social system reinforces rather than restrains the powers
of depersonalisation prevalent in society.

Few are more conscious of these failings of formal education than teachers themselves. Recent history of schooling
provides many examples of genuine attempts on the part of teachers to increase the benefits of institutionalised education by
decreasing its deficiencies. Examples of these attempts range
from such simple matters as the rearrangement of classroom furniture to produce a less formal environment for teaching and
learning, to complex structural changes in the curriculum aimed
at improved learning efficiency. Generally speaking the progressive movement in education in the broadest sense has been
directed at correcting these inadequacies of formal schooling.
Lifelong education serves a similar purpose though its line of
attack is principally through the isolationism of the school
rather than through any one of its deleterious effects.

c) Education for Ever: Education, Schooling and Life

The principles of lifelong education as propounded for example by Lengrand (1970) and Dave (1976), are developed from the
premise that while schooling makes a significant contribution to
education, it should not be identified with it. Education is a
characteristic of living and not just an accompaniment of schooling. This means that the bond between education and life is
immeasurably strengthened and that the purpose of education is
seen more in terms of the amelioration of the human condition
than in terms of academic prowess, paper qualifications, or
social prestige. Education does not start and end with schooling but is an aspect of the continuous process of becoming which
is of the essence of being human.

It is one of the principal tenets of lifelong education
that appropriate opportunities should be available for all
throughout their life-time. This implies that educational provision at any one period should not prejudice an individual's
chances of furthering his educational development at any other
time. To do this lifelong education aims not just to supple-
ment schooling but to transform it. It is in connection with
this process of transformation that the concept of integration
assumes significance for lifelong education.

d) The Relevance of Integration

For a system of lifelong education to operate effectively,
all its constituent parts must work together to further lifelong learning. The contributions of its various agencies must
be so coordinated that the activities of one do not undermine
the potential of another. The isolationist and monopolistic
features of traditional schooling previously referred to constitute a threat to the continuity necessary for lifelong education. Every teacher must therefore be constantly concerned
with the problem of coordinating his particular contribution
to his pupils' education with the contributions made by other
educational agents. This in effect is the problem of integration. It can be tackled in three ways. In the first place
every teacher as a member of a school can consider whether the
work done in the period of schooling helps or hinders the educational development of pupils at other times in their lives.
This aspect of the problem which deals with coordination over
time is referred to as vertical integration (Dave, 1973). Secondly, schools need to match their efforts with those of other
educational agencies at work in the community such as the home

and the mass media (Shimbori, 1975). This is one aspect of what is called horizontal integration. The other, which is the third way of dealing with the problem of integration as a whole, is concerned with articulating the work of teachers themselves particularly across subjects. This is referred to as curriculum integration. Its relevance for lifelong education provides the focus for what follows.

1.3   Significance of Curriculum Integration

Eight of the more important features of curriculum integration are identified and discussed in this section. The reader will note that the issues involved are by no means exclusive to curriculum integration. They are issues in education in general that have particular significance in the context of this study.

a) *Education for Change*

Change is an inevitable accompaniment of life. The extent to which one can adapt to change both in oneself and in society is at least one measure of successful living. This has always been the case, but the problem has been exacerbated of late by the very rapid increase in the rate of change due very largely to developments in science and technology.

As Cropley (1977) observes, the role of the school in a changing world is a crucial issue in education. It used to be that schools could prepare their pupils for life by providing them with the knowledge and skills known to be relevant for living in a comparatively stable society. Such knowledge and skills had been tried and tested by past generations and teachers assumed that because others had found them valid and useful, they were bound to be so for their pupils. This retrospective orientation through which the lessons of the past are assumed to be adequate for the problems of the future, while perhaps appropriate for a stable world, is of little value in a situation of rapid change.

Schools, by their very nature, tend to be traditional in outlook, whereas society is subject to a continual process of change. The slowness of the reaction of the one to the speed of change in the other produces a cultural lag which is characteristic of school education. This is due to two factors which reflect differing attitudes to knowledge in school and society.

The first is the resistance of the curriculum to change and the second the tendency for knowledge to expand. Knowledge that is taught tends to be static; knowledge that is used tends to be dynamic. This hiatus between learning and doing presents the pupil with a continual dilemma, especially since a great deal of what is learned in school will never be realised in action.

Integrated approaches to learning can be helpful in coping with these difficulties. Knowledge that is integrated is much less constrained by its own cognitive structures than knowledge that is narrowly organised on a subject basis. This makes it more flexible but less stable. The integrated curriculum can therefore act as a vehicle by means of which the rapid changes in society can be mediated through the educational system.

One of the concomitants of change has been a vast increase in the sheer quantity of knowledge. Integration can be used to enable teachers to cope with this knowledge explosion. The pressures on the time-table and the amount of knowledge available for teaching and learning are forcing teachers to investigate alternative pedagogical patterns and procedures. The grouping of subjects in common clusters, for example science rather than physics, chemistry and biology, and the teaching of subjects on the basis of key concepts rather than factual information are possibilities open to the teacher using integrative techniques.

Thus curriculum integration is one way to meet the challenge offered to formal schooling by today's rapidly changing world.

b) *School and Society*

The dissociation of school and society, is a central concern of education and implies the separation of learning and living. Traditionally learning is assumed to take place in school and living to occur in society. Though this is a spurious distinction the tension between school and society persists and is reflected in three ways pertinent to this discussion.

In the first place, though school is a part of society, the two often represent different value systems. The school with its academic and intellectual tradition has a tendency to stress intrinsic values, whereas society, involved as it is in the practical situations of life, has a more utilitarian orientation. A consequence of this dichotomy is the frequent dis-

regard for practical application in school learning and the
indifference often encountered among practical people towards
theory. Learning and doing in real terms, however, are complementary activities and learning that extends from birth to
death cannot stand aloof from the practical context of life.
Learning which is unrelated to reality is as useless as doing
which is unrefined by thought. Integration, as will be shown,
operates in the curriculum context as an effective form of
mediation between these divergent systems. It does this by promoting practical learning through which the pupil creates his
own cognitive structures rather than receives them as abstract
concepts from the teacher.

Secondly, society is often thought to represent the world
of work and school the world of learning. There is evidence of
growing concern in many different parts of the world, and particularly in rural, developing countries, about the ill effects
of this dichotomy. Reports of two recent Unesco conferences,
one on secondary education and the world of work (Unesco, 1975b)
and the other on curriculum development for work-oriented education (Unesco, 1976b) highlight some of the difficulties in this
area and record some of the attempts being made to achieve
closer alignment of school and work. There is not an easy answer to this kind of problem but one of the basic principles
underlying most suggested solutions would seem to be the idea
of greater integration between work and learning activities
within the school and work and educational practices within the
community. Such a principle finds strong support in the literature of curriculum integration.

The third distinction, which is not unrelated to the second, is that between formal and informal learning (Scribner and
Cole, 1973). School is the home of formal learning, society
the sphere of informal learning. Part of the purpose of the
progressive movement in education during this century has been
to introduce into schools some of the benefits of the less formal, more experience - centred educational situations that are
to be found in society. While it would be unwise to assume too
tight a relationship between integrated and progressive methods,
there is no denying that integration has assisted in the removal
of a great deal of formality in schools. The integrated day,
for example, attempts to replicate in the classroom something of
the informality of the educational atmosphere of the home, and
the project method replaces the formality of text-book learning
with experience of the actual realities of the external world.

c)   Open Education

Schooling as presently organised represents a closed system of education. This means that the availability of many of
the benefits of education is so controlled that there are very
strict limits on the extent to which many people can take ad-
vantage of them. This control is exercised to a very large
extent through the selective nature of the educational system
and the restrictions placed on the accessibility of knowledge
by subject specialisms.

Despite the move towards a comprehensive system of education in countries like Britain, schooling is still organised on
a selective basis. Comprehensive schools have not removed
elitism; they have only made less obvious the ways in which it
is achieved. The result is still a pyramidal structure of educational advancement characterised by levels of drop-out which
reflect the vocational roles and social status of various
classes in society. Educationally speaking the rich man is
still in his castle and the poor man at his gate.

Many attempts have been made over the years to get round
this problem. The growing emphasis on preschool education attempts to ensure that children from impoverished backgrounds do
not enter the system severely disadvantaged. Alternative routes
to examination success provide opportunities for those who do
not quite make it at school. And various forms of further,
higher and adult education make further progress possible for
many. Despite all these efforts however, the basic disadvantages of the system remain and remind educators of their continuing responsibility for the democratisation of education.

Teachers also exercise control of education through the
organisation of knowledge on a subject basis. Sociologists
such as Young (1971) are at pains to point out that knowledge
is socially constructed and that subjects reflect social behaviour rather than objective reality. Subject specialisms
are therefore basically groups of people who have organised
themselves into professional guilds which have their own value
systems, rules of membership and modes of behaviour. They
operate in schools in ways which promote their own interests
and strengthen their control over a particular area of knowledge. They do this by securing sufficient territorial rights
within the curriculum to further their subject, by prolonging
the period of initiation into the mysteries of the subject, and
by restricting entry to the specialist elite to those who can

most fully satisfy the conditions of membership. Young argues
that this produces a curriculum which is imposed on children
on the basis of teacher self-interest, is dissociated from the
real world and therefore a source of alienation.

There are several ways in which the various forms of curriculum integration can encourage a more open approach to school
education. By placing a particular emphasis on cooperative
forms of teaching and learning, integrated methods not only
open up lines of communication between subjects but require a
considerable degree of pupil participation in the planning and
implementation of the curriculum. They break down some of the
barriers of academicism by adopting a functional rather than a
structural approach to knowledge. And they demystify knowledge
by revealing the deep structures of subjects much earlier in
the learning process than is usual in formal subject teaching
(Bernstein, 1971). But the extent to which they do all these
things depends, of course, on the particular method employed
and the attitudes and abilities of the teachers involved.

d) Knowledge that is Useful

Knowledge is one of the principal resources used by
schools. The kind of knowledge and the use made of it deter-
mines the quality of the education offered. The formal, academic tradition in school education has tended to stress theoretical rather than practical knowledge - knowing that instead
of knowing how - with the result that a great deal of what has
been taught in schools has had no use or relevance for living.

There are several reasons for this. In the first place
teachers are, by the very nature of their job, predisposed
towards theory rather than practice. Even knowledge of a practical kind tends in the formal teaching situation to be reduced
to theory. Thus teachers are to be found, for example, talking
about trees from textbooks when these very same trees are to be
found growing in the school playground. Secondly, the tradition of classical learning in western education dies hard. It
fostered what might be called the cult of the remote. In this
tradition the content of teaching was often far removed in both
space and time from the situation of those who were learning it.
The life of Cincinnatus is a far cry from life in Cincinnati!
Such a temptation to distance learning from reality is ever
present in teaching. Thirdly, schools are never at the fron-
tiers of knowledge and what they teach is inevitably tinged
with a certain obsolescence. Teaching is strongly retrospec-

tive in orientation and pupils are often expected to learn
through other people's discoveries rather than through their
own. School knowledge tends to be second-hand and out-of-date
knowledge.

At a time when teachers are faced with an abundance of
knowledge and a choice of curriculum provision, the opportunity
to incorporate in the curriculum knowledge that can be used by
children to improve the quality of their lives has never been
greater. One way of doing this is through revision of subject
curricula, for subjects as such are not incapable of practical
application. Another way is through integrated teaching, many
forms of which are characterised by a greater practicability
than formal teaching of subjects.

The ways that integrated teaching can promote practicability will be discussed in detail later, but it may be helpful at
this stage to mention three of them briefly. Firstly, many of
the topics covered in integrated teaching are concerned with
problems in the contemporary world such as those of nutrition,
population, pollution, prejudice and peace. These are not theoretical notions of interest only to academics, but practical
matters of concern to all. Secondly, many forms of integrated
teaching often take the form of practical activities outside
school or work with practical materials in the classroom. Thus
a project on, say, water, could involve a visit to a reservoir,
periodic measurement of rainfall, testing for hardness or soft-
ness of water, or experiments to discover the effects of water
on plant life. Thirdly, a number of integrated approaches involve a practical approach to the learning of even theoretical
notions. They advocate learning by doing where at all possible.
Thus an infant school which is organised on the basis of an
integrated day, provides children with a learning environment
in which even a theoretical subject like mathematics can be
taught through practical activities.

Curriculum integration thus provides teaching and learning with a practical orientation which usefully compensates for
the theoretical emphasis frequently found in formal subject
approaches. In this respect it helps to make knowledge useful
for living.

e) Operational Learning

It is a commonly held view that one of the principal functions of schools is to provide pupils with the knowledge and

skills thought to be necessary for living in the adult world. Though the rapid advances in knowledge and the changing nature of society make it difficult for schools to fulfil this function adequately, schools are still seen as guardians of a cultural heritage which they bequeath to our children in order to prepare them for life. Transmission of knowledge is still regarded as a prime function of schooling.

The objections to it, are not based entirely on the idea of the obsolescence of knowledge but on other changes in knowledge and the ways in which it is learned.

Formal schooling has relied very heavily on the idea that knowledge is content to be learned, information provided by the teacher and assimilated by the pupil. The difficulty with this idea is not just that it separates what is knows from ways of knowing but that it also dissociates knowledge from the practical experience from which it is derived. Learning becomes an activity concerned with schooling rather than related to life, a way of coping with teachers rather than a way of dealing with experience.

In recent years many educators have attempted to overcome these difficulties by emphasising the methodological rather than the substantive aspects of knowledge. This has meant that the focus has changed from teaching, in the formal sense, to learning as an operational and not just an acquisitional process. There are two aspects to this. In the first place, learning a subject is now seen to involve an understanding of the basic principles and procedures of the subject rather than assimilation of the factual matter produced by the application of these principles and procedures. And secondly, it is now realised that learning is an aspect of behaviour that needs to be understood in itself and that learning how to learn is just as important as learning what can be known. In other words the process of learning has as much significance as its content (Biggs, 1973).

Many forms of curriculum integration support this notion of operational learning. For the present, two examples will be given. Firstly, subjects which share common principles and procedures are often subsumed under the broader heading of a discipline and taught in an integrated way. These principles and procedures are quite central to many forms of integrated teaching. Secondly, teaching children how to learn involves socio-affective as well as cognitive considerations and these

are a feature of the kind of learning environment often associated with integrated approaches. The emphasis is often upon
practical and participatory forms of teaching and learning. In
such respects, therefore, curriculum integration promotes a
view of learning as a function in life rather than a feature of
schooling.

f) Consensus for Action

Educational systems generally are both fragmented and
dissociative. They separate school and society, learning and
living, general and vocational education, formal and informal
teaching. They dissociate the arts and the sciences, the moral
and the technical, the religious and the secular. They find
difficulty in providing for the whole man and for different
aspects of his development. While it is desirable that any system should cater for these many different aspects of life, it
is important that it should do so in a concerted and coordinated
manner.

It is this kind of thinking that underlies the concepts
of vertical and horizontal integration. They imply that some
kind of consensus for action is necessary if the priority in
education is to be the welfare of pupils.

Curriculum integration operates in two ways to open up
the lines of communication between different educational agencies and achieve some consensus for action. First of all the
logic of the notion presupposes some form of unity of purpose
and action on the part of teachers. Without this unity of purpose in the curriculum context the academic world would degen-
erate into the scholarly equivalent of a tribal society. One
of the principal dangers of the traditional, subject-centred
approach lies in the temptation that is ever present for the
teacher to strive for the self-perpetuation of his subject
rather than for the self-enhancement of his pupil. Integration
to some extent minimises this danger. It not only forces teachers to cross the boundaries of subjects, but it also encourages them to consider the kinds of contribution that different
subjects make to the educational development of children. At
the operational level it is also claimed, for example by Bernstein (1971), that while subject teaching encourages proliferation of teaching practices in that it allows each teacher to
act on his own, integrated teaching represents a movement towards a common pedagogy and homogeneity in performance. This
does not imply that integrated teaching is more stereotyped

than subject teaching. The variety of approaches available to teachers in the integrated situation is as great, if not greater, than that available to subject teachers. Bernstein's point is that teachers are much more likely to act in concert in the integrated classroom than when teaching on their own. To do this they must obviously plan their work together. The importance of such unity of action at the planning stage for the development of an integrated curriculum is stressed by Lawton (1969).

Secondly, as has already been indicated, integrated approaches have the effect of breaking down the barriers between school and society and opening up the lines of communication between teachers and those persons and agencies outside the school that fulfil an educational function. No more need be said about this at this stage.

g) *The Primacy of the Person*

Schools serve three main functions. The first is an academic function. Schools act as one of the principal retail outlets for knowledge. The second is a social function. They organise and administer education on institutional lines to meet the needs of society. And the third is a personal function. They are there to facilitate the educational development of the individual.

This third function is the most important of the three and the other two should be subservient to it. When this fails to happen then school education suffers from two serious defects. These occur when either or both of the other two functions become dominant. Over-emphasis on the first results in an academic form of education in which other-than-cognitive aspects of the personality are neglected. Over-emphasis on the second produces a dehumanised form of education in which the person becomes the slave of the system. Stress on all-round personality development and the individualisation of learning, two ideals which find sympathetic support in the idea of curriculum integration, serves to counteract these dangers.

1) *Personality Development*

Education as the development of the whole person is a well established educational ideal, though one difficult to achieve in practice, particularly in the formal setting of the school where the significance of intellectual ability is often

over emphasised. Such a comprehensive approach to the education of the individual involves not just the nurture of different aspects of personality but their effective coordination
in the development of an integrated person. Harmony within
the individual and between the individual and his environment
is an important goal to be achieved through education (Cropley,
1976; Vaideanu, 1976).

It is the teacher's task to promote development with this
concept in mind and this involves deliberate effort aimed at
assisting pupils to acquire a coherent view of life. It is of
interest to note that a writer such as Jeffreys (1962) maintains
that such an undertaking involves two things. The first is a
belief in the sacredness of human personality which he considers
to be a master concept that is not only generally acceptable,
but one that can act as a principle of coherence for our thought
and knowledge. The other is an understanding of the interrelationship of the different areas of thought and knowledge, by
which he means an appreciation of the kind of contribution that
they severally make to the human outlook. The principle of
integration is thus firmly rooted in the concept of personality
and the process of education.

2) Individualisation of Learning

The opportunity to enhance one's education should be ever
present throughout life and available in whatever form of organisation is necessary. At no point in life should anyone be
either locked into any system detrimental to his educational
development or out of any system conducive to it.

One of the disadvantages of the school system is that it
imposes a pre-cast curriculum on pupils irrespective of their
individual talents and interests. This means that the child
is to some extent geared to the system and constrained by it.
He has little opportunity to individualise his own learning.

Many developments in education in recent years have been
aimed at solving this problem. The extreme solution is to allow the child to develop his own curriculum under the guidance
of his teachers but attempts in this direction have sometimes
had undesirable consequences (Auld, 1976). Though it is possible to individualise learning within subject areas, many
forms of individualised learning involve some degree of integration. Such approaches usually provide opportunity for the pupil to exercise considerable responsibility for his own learn-

ing. This is particularly the case in those examples of integration which involve the child in activity, enquiry or first-
hand experience.

h) The Enhancement of Educability

Implicit in such a personalised approach to education is
an unfaltering faith in the enduring educability of the individual and in the individual's potential for self-realisation.
The teacher must therefore always act on the assumption that
there are no barriers to the progressive self-enhancement of
his pupils except when helping them to surmount them.

A useful distinction can be made between manifest and
latent educability for it is one that is allied to certain of
the distinguishing features of subject-centred as distinct from
integrated teaching.

1) Manifest Educability

Formal systems of education such as are found in schools
set limits to the educability of a large percentage of the population by means of examinations, for these are used for the
most part to segregate the able from the less able, that is as
a means of social engineering rather than educational advancement, except, of course, for the fortunate few. In general
terms it is assumed that the manifest educability of examination candidates is highly correlated with their latent educability as individuals. This may be a valid judgement within the
constraints of the examination situation, but in the broader
perspective of the life of the individual it may be little more
than an impediment to progress.

A further feature of examinations tends to support this
view. Their principal function is to test ability for dealing
with theory rather than judge potential for learning how to
deal with real-life situations.

Since examinations are very closely tied to subject differentiation, the concept of manifest educability is one that
is more strongly linked to subject-based rather than integrated
teaching.

2) Latent Educability

The concept of latent educability cuts through these bar-

riers set up by institutionalised education. It does not accept that manifest ability displaced in largely theoretical
examinations is a true test of latent ability for learning, nor
does it concede that the essence of education lies in the ac-
quisition of content. It rejects the idea of education as a
basis for social class and the materialistic view of knowledge
as a possession, a sort of mental property to be acquired as a
status symbol of the consumer society. Instead it views education as the enhancement of educability rather than the transmission of content, that is as process rather than product.

        This has implications for both pupil and teacher. For
the pupil the process of learning becomes more important than
the content of learning. Learning does not become content-less
but content assumes a functional rather than a substantive role.
Instead of learning content, pupils learn how to learn through
content. The structure, skills and competencies inherent in
content become the means of educational development (Lamm, 1969).
The ultimate aim of integrative learning according to Connelly
(1972), is to enable the child to become his own educator.

        In such circumstances the role of the teacher also changes.
His concern for the pupil is personalised. Neither can remain
units in a system but must become persons in a relationship.
The teacher's job is not just to see his pupils through examinations but to help them on their way in life. He ceases to be
the purveyor of pre-packaged information and becomes a facilitator of learning. By being integrated into the learning community of the classroom, he becomes responsible for an approach
to learning which has many of the hall-marks of integrated
teaching.

1.4   The Prospect of Mutual Support

        The foregoing discussion has brought to light a number of
educational ideas put forward by the advocates of curriculum
integration which find support in the literature of lifelong
education. They put the person and not the system at the centre
of education; they advocate a greater cohesion of school and
society; they recognise the inevitability and ubiquity of change;
they recommend an open and practical approach to teaching and
learning; and they view education as a cooperative enterprise
requiring the coordination of the efforts of all those who
contribute to it.

The two notions, however, have separate histories in educational thought and practice and are relatively independent.

Recent analyses of lifelong education suggest that curriculum integration may have considerable relevance for lifelong education despite their independent histories.

It will be recalled that lifelong education is basically idealistic in nature. In the literature it is presented as a set of principles for organising education, guidelines for planning and implementing the curriculum, and values for determining the direction of educational development. What it seems to lack is a set of existing practices that exemplify it in operation. This may be due to the fact that such practices have yet to be identified, or that those that are relevant require modification.

The phrase 'curriculum integration', on the other hand, refers to a set of educational practices which have been developed largely on the basis of teachers' dissatisfaction with the increasing fragmentation of the school curriculum, their unease about the dissociation of what is taught in school and what is experienced in life, their despair at the practical difficulties raised by the proliferation of knowledge, and so on. Though each of these practices may have some theoretical justification, curriculum integration in general lacks an overall, theoretical rationale. Such a rationale would, for example, help to clarify what is meant by curriculum integration, its relationship to subject teaching, the forms that it takes, the purposes it serves, when and to whom it is applicable, and its repercussions on classroom teaching and school organisation. At present curriculum integration tends to be self-justifying and a more realistic appraisal of its potential might be possible were it viewed from the perspective of lifelong education.

The existence of common purposes as identified in this chapter suggests that juxtaposing the two could have mutually beneficial results. In the case of lifelong education, its analytical and coordinating values are qualified by the extent to which the reforms advocated are capable of being implemented. What is needed are educational practices exemplifying and illustrating some of the essential features of lifelong education. In addition to expounding the principles of lifelong education it is necessary to ask if practices exist which put these principles into effect, even if the practices in question were adopted without explicit reference to lifelong education. Dis-

covery of such practices would help to give an air of practical-
ity to lifelong education, and add validity to the statements
made by theorists.

In the case of curriculum integration, the problem is the
reverse. Many practices exist but they have been introduced on
a piecemeal basis and for reasons that have often been question-
able. Lifelong education would appear to provide some theoretical support for the idea of curriculum integration, focus attention on what may be its key features, and, rather than leave
it as an end in itself, give it greater purpose in the wider
context of education.

It is with these possibilities in mind that the following
chapters have been written.

CHAPTER 2

THE NATURE AND VARIETIES
OF CURRICULUM INTEGRATION

The concept of curriculum integration incorporates many different ideas and a variety of practices. In this chapter an attempt will be made to uncover its essential meanings and describe and appraise the different ways in which it can be operated.

2.1   The Nature of Curriculum Integration

a)   Different Views of Integration

There is no one, generally accepted view of the nature of integration. Its uncertain function in the structure of knowledge, the different degrees to which it can be applied, the many ways in which it can be practised, its variable status in the curriculum, its changing relevance for different age groups, the range of attitudes towards it, all render it a difficult concept to define.

For some, integration is a social phenomenon, a reflection in school of changing patterns of power and authority in society (Bernstein (1), 1967); for others it is an administrative device, a way of organising the timetable to cope with the expansion of knowledge (Morris, 1970). For some it is a problem-centred ac-

---

[1] The references in this paragraph do not imply that the authors quoted necessarily hold these views. Some may do, but in most cases they are named as authorities who report that such views exist. Also the fact that they are attached to particular viewpoints does not exclude them from subscribing to others.

tivity (Bolam, 1970/1), for others a child-centred approach
(Gwynn and Chase, 1969). For some it characterises the initial
stages in learning (Pring, 1971); for others it complements differentiation as a cognitive activity (Moulez, 1973). For some
it is a way of making the theoretical practical (Blum, 1973),
for others a way of making education purposeful (Acland, 1967).
For some it is a characteristic of curriculum planning (Lawton,
1975), for others a feature of productive thinking (Taba, 1962).
For some it makes subjects subservient to a relational idea
(Bernstein, 1971); for others it makes subject content subservient to intellectual skill (Tawney, 1975). For some it derives
from a belief in the unity of knowledge (Levit, 1971), for
others from the inevitability of its fragmentation (James, 1968).
Some imply that it is a characteristic of some subjects but not
others (Hirst, 1974); others claim that is is necessary because
of the existence of all subjects (Owens, 1972).

The ways in which people view its implementation are no
less varied. Lancashire (1973) differentiates between integration which is hierarchical and integration which is lateral.
The former involves the arrangement of subjects in larger and
larger groups; botany, for example, becomes part of biology and
biology becomes part of science. Rather than give each of these
sciences a place on the time-table and teach them separately,
teachers can use their interrelationship as a basis for an integrated course in, say, biological science. If a wider range of
scientific subjects were used, the course could be simply a
course in science. Lateral integration on the other hand refers
to relationships between subjects which share and contribute to
a common area of interest. A topic on houses, for example,
could incorporate contributions from architecture, mathematics,
geography, history, sociology, art, science and many other subjects.

Skilbeck (1972) identifies three levels of integration.
The first is integration at the subject level. Subjects themselves are not only integrated systems of thought but are, as
Zverev (1975) observes, also the source of the links that can
be formed with other subjects. The second level is that of
interdisciplinary cooperation in which the logical coherence of
the separate disciplines is respected. An example would be an
environmental studies programme consisting of contributions
from geography, history and science. At the third level the
disciplines lose their separate identities and are replaced by
a new form of the organisation of knowledge based on, say, psychological rather than logical principles. Some types of thema-

tic approaches or core programmes would fall into this category.

Quite a different form of categorisation is referred to by Kooi (1975). She distinguishes between a conceptual approach to curriculum integration in which the focus is upon major concepts, for example the concept of man, an environmental approach which operates on the basis of environmental problems, for example pollution, and a process approach which promotes particular disciplinary processes, such as the processes of science.

A further distinction is made by Lynch (1977) between integration as the synthetic creation of a whole from parts and integration as the principle governing the relationship of parts within a whole. It will be shown, for example on page 34, that different ways of integrating knowledge are based on this distinction. An integrated curriculum can be constructed either by interrelating various subjects as they exist, for example combining geography and history under an environmental studies heading, or by starting with a global concept such as man and his environment, deciding what needs to be taught about it, and borrowing material from various subjects, if and when necessary, to help in teaching it. In the one case the differentiated structure of knowledge with its multiplicity of subjects is the starting point, in the other it is a general idea which may prompt teachers to organise knowledge relevant to it in a way quite unrelated to subjects. It is of interest to note that the latter approach in particular provides opportunity not only for interrelating material from different subjects but also for incorporating knowledge that might not be found in school textbooks.

These different views provide a range of ideas from which a number of characteristic features of curriculum integration can be deduced.

b) Subjects, Disciplines and Integration

Perhaps the most important feature of integration is the nature of its relationship with subjects and disciplines. It is sometimes assumed that integration is an either/or matter, an alternative to or substitute for subject teaching. This implies that the two stand in a polarized relationship and are to be thought of as opposites. Such a view is quite mistaken for at least two reasons. In the first place integration and differentiation are not opposites but correlatives, that is the meaning of the one is partly dependent upon its association

with the other. The notions, therefore, are complementary and
not contradictory. And secondly, both analysis and synthesis
are integral to the processes of learning and thinking (Ausubel,
1967). The one cannot really be employed without the other.

The confusion arising from the relationship between integrated teaching and subject teaching is exacerbated by a further complication. While integration and differentiation are
correlative, integration and subjects are not. Integration is
a process, subjects are a product. Integrated teaching and
subject teaching are not different but represent two stages of
the same process. Subject teaching is a form of integrated
teaching. To teach a subject is to teach an integrated cognitive structure (Bruner, 1960).

The validity of this argument is strengthened by a consideration of the difference between subjects and disciplines.
Disciplines are more highly structured, more closely integrated
cognitive patterns than subjects. They represent the functional
more than the substantive side of the cognitive coin. They are
ways of knowing rather than forms of knowledge. They represent
processes of thinking rather than products of thought. They
involve modes of enquiry, conceptual principles and methods of
evaluation that are characterised by a permanence and a stabi-
lity, both within the learner and within culture, which often
eludes mere factual knowledge. Furthermore they represent the
significant dimensions of human experience and the principal
modes of consciouness characteristic of man. At the heart of
the disciplines lie the archetypal dichotomies of subject and
object, quality and quantity, particular and general, thought
and action, reason and emotion, that underpin the structure of
knowledge. This is what integration is about.

The problem at the curriculum level arises not because
subjects and disciplines are not integrative but for two other
quite different reasons. The first is that the human mind becomes thwarted in its effort to construct and maintain a coherent view of life in the face of the sheer quantity of human
knowledge, its steadily increasing rate of expansion, and the
forever changing images of reality which it presents. The second is that the intellectual structuring and administrative
transformation of knowledge that occur in the curriculum, not
only stop the integrative process activated in subjects and
disciplines in its tracks, but also increase the difficulty of
maintaining appropriate rhythmic interaction of differentiation
and integration at all times in the life of the individual and

particularly during the school years.

The implementation of curriculum measures to counteract these difficulties creates for teachers a further dilemma not unrelated to the product-process ambivalence encountered previously. In the context of lifelong education most would concur with Dressel (1958) that what they are striving for is the creation of an integrative person rather than simply the presentation of an integrated curriculum. The aim of the integrated approach is to ensure the integrity of the personality and, hopefully, one way of doing this is to present our pupils with integrated material for study. The latter is but the instrument of a higher ideal, and it will be part of the purpose of this study to show that its influence on the teaching situation as a whole suggests that it can usefully assist in the fulfilment of other important conditions for the achievement of that ideal.

In the context of this study integration will be considered to refer to particular ways of organising knowledge for curriculum purposes that counteract the tendency for knowledge to become fragmented and irrelevant, and assist pupils in developing and maintaining a coherent view of life. The variety of ways in which this can be done is our immediate concern.

2.2   The Varieties of Curriculum Integration

The above analysis provides some useful categories for the construction of a typology of curriculum integration which is outlined in Table 2.1. The purpose of such a classification is not to collect and list all the possible variations but to identify the main dimensions, the different levels and the principal types of curriculum integration. Used as cognitive stencil to locate particular varieties of course or nomenclature, it will be found to be wanting, for many of the different approaches to curriculum integration often contribute to more than one of the category levels. Provided this caveat is heeded, the typology may have its use in planning or evaluating integrated curricula.

Table 2.1
A Typology of Curriculum Integration

1) STRUCTURAL TYPES: which may be:

    a) *Quantitative:* based on the process of:

           1) *Summation*
           2) *Contribution*

    b) *Qualitative:* based on the process of:

           1) *Fusion*
           2) *Synthesis:* which can be of four types:

                    i) *Linear*
                  ii) *Cyclical*
                iii) *Methodological*
                 iv) *Holistic*

2) FUNCTIONAL TYPES: which may be:

    a) *Intrinsic:*   involving integrative learning through:

           1) *Needs and Interests*
           2) *Activity*
           3) *Enquiry*
           4) *Experience*

    b) *Extrinsic:*   involving:

           1) *Inductive (Problem) Approaches*
           2) *Deductive (Teleological) Approaches*

In each case variations in scale are possible.

a) *Structural and Functional Types* (1)

In the structural category integration is conceived as a reorganisation of the structure of knowledge within the curriculum; in the functional category knowledge is viewed as a resource to be used for the promotion of integrative experiences. This distinction is similar to that made by Bellack and Kliebard (1971) between organised knowledge curricula and directly functional curricula. It comprises the distinction previously made between forms of integration based on the restructuring of knowledge and those devised for the purpose of facilitating integrative learning. The one is integration which is teacher-centred; the other is integration which is pupil-centred. The one follows from logical and epistemological considerations, the other from psychological or social considerations.

b) *Structural Types: Quantitative and Qualitative*

The structural category is divisible in terms of those forms of integration which involve juxtaposition of subject elements and those which involve reorganised disciplinary material. The difference is between weak and strong forms of integration, between material which at the one extreme is presented consecutively on a modular-type basis, and at the other is so organised that the disciplinary contributions are made in a more concurrent and unified form. This is the distinction between quantitative and qualitative structural types.

In quantitative forms of integration the structures of the disciplines are respected and they each make their individual contribution almost independently of the other; in qualitative forms the material is organised on the basis of some common structural principle. This principle is derived from the subjects or disciplines concerned, rather than from any function they may serve in integrative learning. The notion of set in mathematics, or of form in the arts, or of power in the social sciences, for example, are logical derivatives from the disciplines rather than psychological devices for furthering knowledge and understanding, though of course they can be used for this purpose.

---

1 Because of the nature of the discussion which follows, the numbers and letters in the headings do not correspond with those in the typology.

The notions of breadth and depth of knowledge are not unrelated to this distinction between quantitative and qualitative
structural integration. Quantitative integration can involve
quite simply an increase in the number of subjects or disciplines contributing to a learning experience thus providing a
broader curriculum perspective. Qualitative integration on the
other hand promotes greater depth of understanding, being concerned with key concepts and general principles inherent in the
disciplines. These lie not at the surface level of factual information but are the integrative threads which hold the structure together as a discipline (Bloom, 1958). Such threads are
related more to the methodology of the subject than to its content. Bernstein (1971) argues that it is this penetration of
the deep structures of the disciplines that is one of the distinguishing features of integrated teaching. Though these integrative threads can be functionally employed in learning, they
are essentially a structural creation of the teacher devised to
present a coherent view of knowledge, rather than a functional
device for promoting integrative ability. They can be used for
functional purposes but need not be.

c) *Quantitative Structural Types: Summation Category*

The most elementary form of curriculum integration occurs
when two or more subject areas are no longer taught separately
but are linked together to form a more comprehensive unit. Often the most obvious effect of this sort of linkage is in the
wording of the time-table, where a broad term replaces two or
more narrower ones. The term 'mathematics', for example, is
now frequently used in place of arithmetic, algebra, geometry
and trigonometry. And for some time now a general term such as
'language' has been used to cover the various aspects of speaking, writing, comprehension and grammar. While few teachers
would describe such a course in mathematics or language as integrated, some developments in fields such as science and social
studies are sometimes so described (Ross et al., 1975). Biology and geography, for example, can be combined in an environmental science course, and history, geography and religious education subsumed under the more general heading of social
studies. In many instances the end result is often little different from what was taught previously, especially when the
separate elements are taught by different teachers. The use of
the term 'integrated' in these cases may be related to the
scale of such developments; those in science and social studies
involve links between a large number of quite extensive subject
areas. Many courses described as interdisciplinary are of this

summative type. They comprise the sum total of separate contributions from different areas of knowledge.

   d) *Quantitative Structural Types: Contribution Category*

   The idea of contribution, sometimes described as correla-
tion, implies a closer link than that of summation or combination. Whereas courses can be combined simply by rearranging
the subject matter, to be correlated they require to have some
common element to which each can contribute. They must have a
mutual bearing on one another (Gwynn and Chase, 1969). Thus a
teacher of literature might enlist the help of a history colleague to provide background, or of a theological colleague to
elucidate the religious ideas of certain literary works. Or a
primary school teacher might involve an engineer to provide
specialist information on, say, textile or agricultural machin-
ery. This kind of contributive activity can help to fill in
gaps left by purely subject teaching and to extend and reinforce
knowledge by approaching it from different angles. Any good
primary school teacher who has to cover a vast range of subjects
is well practised in this kind of cross-fertilisation of ideas.

   Some forms of core curricula are of the contribution type,
though the term core has many other more extensive meanings.
In this instance one subject becomes the focus of the total curriculum and all other subjects are contributory to it. Theology played this role at one time and it has been suggested that
other subjects such as history, or social studies might also do
so. This type of interrelationship would not be generally fa-
voured today because it would not only produce a surfeit of
teaching in one subject, but also make the teaching in all other
subjects subordinate to it.

   e) *Qualitative Structural Types: Fusion Category*

   The concept of fusion marks a significant departure from
the previous two concepts of summation and contribution. It is
not concerned simply with either the reorganisation of content
in two or more subjects, or with supplementing course content
in one subject by course content from another. Rather it involves the construction of a teaching programme based on some
over-arching principle, some common issue, some mutual area of
interest. Oliver (1968) points out that though the term 'fusion' is sometimes applied to courses which involve only a quantitative form of structural integration, the real significance
of the term resides in the extent to which it signifies a move

away from the subject-centred curriculum. It involves blending,
not just juxtaposition. Yet it barely fulfils the conditions
of true synthesis. Its topic-centred approach brings it close
to certain functional types, but it is structural rather than
functional because its primary concern is the structuring of
knowledge rather than the nurturing of integrity.

A course in mathematics or biology, for instance, taught
as a unified programme and not just as a series of separate
units from each of the contributory subjects, would come into
this category. Also included would be certain forms of topic
or project work with a didactic emphasis. A topic on trees,
for example, could be taught in this way using a variety of insights from different areas of knowledge.

f) Qualitative Structural Types: Synthesis Category

At this level of integration the teacher is concerned
with the warp and woof of the fabric of knowledge and not so
much with individual subjects, or even disciplines, and their
common areas of interest. Synthesis involves the uncovering of
common concepts, the detection of shared meanings, the comparison of different ways of knowing, the interpretation of different approaches to reality, the appraisal of different value
judgements, the evaluation of different ways of finding out
what there is to be known. Synthesis is not a matter of seeing
the whole of knowledge from one point of view or asserting a
belief in the unity of knowledge in the face of its manifest
diversity (Tyler, 1958). Rather it is an approach to knowledge
which recognises both the differences and similarities in phenomena, which sees both the merits and limitations of different
modes of discovery, which uses these modes in ways appropriate
to the phenomena concerned, which can modify its conceptual
structure in the light of new knowledge, and which can differentiate between meaningful reality and its transient representa-
tions in the mind. Within the curriculum there are four ways
in which synthesis can be achieved.

1) Linear Synthesis

This involves grouping the various subjects of the curriculum in categories which represent different logical structures, different ways of knowing (Hirst, 1974) or different aspects of culture (Lawton, 1969). It is a method that is based
on the premise that the principles of integration are inherent
in the structure of knowledge since knowledge is the publicly

accepted symbolic representation of experience.

One attempt to structure the curriculum on this basis is
that of Hirst (1974). He distinguishes between forms and fields
of knowledge. Forms of knowledge are discrete logical structures with their own distinctive concepts and procedures which,
together, constitute rational thinking and represent experience.
They are mathematics, the physical sciences, ethics, religion,
aesthetics and possibly history and the human sciences. Hirst
maintains that these are not subjects but disciplines, being
concerned with the activity of knowing rather than with the
content of knowledge. They thus represent internally coherent
aspects of experience all of which are necessary for educational
development. Fields of knowledge, on the other hand, are areas
of subject matter that cross the boundaries of the forms and
derive their logical criteria from them. They represent the
integration of knowledge from the forms and include subject
areas such as geography, engineering and medicine as well as
certain types of project work carried out in schools. From an
integration point of view the difficulty with Hirst's scheme is
that, while it integrates some subjects within certain disciplines and some forms within fields, it offers no solution to
the problems of the integration of the disciplines themselves
and of the fields derived from them.

Lawton (1969) tackles the same problem from a sociologi-
cal point of view. He believes that children should be introduced in school to significant aspects of our common culture.
The curriculum which he proposes respects the individuality of
subjects but recognises their interrelatedness. It consists of
the following five cores: mathematics, the sciences, the humanities, the expressive arts and moral education. The humanities,
for example, would include history, geography, classical studies,
the social sciences, literature and religious studies. Though
each core would be distinct and internally integrated, the curriculum would allow for the possibility of demonstrating the
interrelatedness of the various cores. Mathematics is clearly
a tool of the sciences, and scientific method has its use in
understanding some aspects of our humanity. Like Hirst's,
Lawton's scheme is one in which the various subjects of the
curriculum are brought together in meaningful clusters. The
end result is, however, a much more integrated structure than
the forms and fields of knowledge.

Both these approaches start with the multiplicity of subjects that constitute knowledge and attempt to classify them

into broader categories. Because they regard knowledge as given,
they tend to objectify it. This tendency often has the effect
of dissociating knowledge from experience. Nevertheless what
is significant about these approaches is that they view knowledge as a structured representation of experience, and portray
the curriculum as a cultural representation of knowledge.

2) Cyclical Synthesis

This particular form of integrative approach is concerned
with the selection and presentation of certain aspects of knowledge in ways appropriate to the phases of development of the
growing child. It brings to bear certain features of developmental psychology on the organisation of knowledge in the curriculum. This combination of logical and psychological principles provides the basis for a cyclical form of integrative
teaching and learning which follows the pattern of cognitive
growth.

One example of this type of arrangement is Bruner's (1960)
idea of a spiral curriculum. He argues that a number of fundamental ideas or basic themes lie at the heart of all knowledge.
These should form the basis of any curriculum since they represent issues that society deems important in the education of
its members. Thus ideas such as tragedy in literature or set
in mathematics should be introduced in simple form early in the
education of children and developed on a recurrent basis throughout the period of schooling. By returning to these ideas in
varying contexts and with increasing levels of awareness, children will be encouraged to develop a coherent outlook particularly if the ideas span, as well as penetrate, the disciplines.

An earlier example of cyclical synthesis is to be found
in Whitehead's (1932) concept of rhythm in education. Concerned
about the fragmentation of the curriculum, he starts from the
interesting assertion that the only subject-matter for education is 'life' in all its variety. Both in life and in education as an aspect of life he sees a recurring rhythmic pattern
in which ideas are first of all conceived, then put into some
kind of order in the mind, and subsequently formed into ever-
widening cognitive structures. These stages of intellectual
progress he calls the stage of romance, the stage of precision
and the stage of generalisation. Education consists of the continual recurrence of this cyclic process, both during specific
learning experiences, such as a language lesson in the infant
school, and throughout the various phases of educational devel-

opment in life. The curriculum should be such that it continually promotes the synthesis of thought and ideas that is characteristic of the stage of generalisation.

3) *Methodological Synthesis*

In the case of methodological synthesis the integrating
principle is derived from aspects of the methodology of a subject and the ways in which it can be taught. The principle is
then applied to the teaching of other subjects, thereby providing a certain unity of approach which in many instances can
have a considerable influence on content. The result is integrative because of the blending of ways of knowing which otherwise were thought to be distinct.

Perhaps the best example of this type of integration is
the influence that the idea of creativity has had on education
generally. It originated presumably in the fine arts, but has
been applied to and transformed the teaching of subjects as
diverse as children's writing, physical education and science.
A similar example is the adaptation of the heuristic approach
in science through the use of discovery methods in the primary
school. Both these developments represent attempts to synthe-
sise ways of knowing previously characterised by their distinctiveness rather than their similarity. Their principal weak-
ness lies in the distortion of the teaching of the host discipline, which can result from the over-zealous application of
the other's methodology. Though there are obvious links between these methods and some functional approaches, they remain
structural because their influence is mediated principally
through the reorganisation of content.

4) *Holistic Synthesis*

Whereas previous forms of synthesis are derived from subjects and disciplines as particularities, holistic synthesis
originates in the totality of experience. The synthesis in the
one case stems from interrelating parts, in the other from
interpreting the whole. The one is based on the fragmentation
of knowledge, the other on the unity of experience. The one
is narrowly epistemological, the other more generally philosophical.

This is the kind of distinction that has already been
made in the discussion on page 24. There it was observed that
an integrated curriculum can be provided either by putting dif-

ferent subjects together in a more coherent curriculum package,
or by starting with a general idea or overarching concept and
borrowing material from various subjects to help in teaching it.
Whereas other forms of synthesis are inductive and derive the
general from the particular, holistic synthesis is deductive
since it derives the particular from the general. The general
in every case may not be just one idea but a number of inter-
related ideas which are in themselves coherent. Thus a starting point might be Bruner's (1967) notion of man as course of
study, or the example which was previously given of man and his
environment.

In the literature there are plenty of such universal notions on which a curriculum can be based. The following are
some examples: Snow's (1959) two cultures - the arts and the
sciences; Macmurray's (1936) interpretation of art, science and
religion as the three modes of consciousness characteristic of
man; Rogers' (1964) three ways of knowing - subjective, objective and interpersonal; or Phenix's (1964) six realms of meaning - symbolics (language, mathematics, art), empirics (physical and social sciences), aesthetics (literature, art, music),
synnoetics (literature, philosophy, history, psychology, theology), ethics/morals (philosophy, theology) and synoptics (philosophy, religion, history).

The main feature of these notions is that they are derived
from the unity of experience rather than from the diversity of
subject matter. They provide a coherent framework on which to
build a curriculum. Whatever elements are incorporated in it
will always have a common reference point in the notion from
which they were derived. The notion forms the bond that holds
the curriculum together. It is true, of course, that many of
these notions contain the origins of fragmentation. The distinction between the arts and the sciences or between empirics
and ethics are cases in point. It is because of such distinctions that integration is necessary. The purpose of integration is not to obliterate these distinctions, however, but to
make them meaningful for the lives of individuals. They cannot
be meaningful in the context of life if they remain unrelated
in the context of the curriculum. The chances are that they
are less likely to remain separate in the context of a curriculum structured on the basis of some common principle, than in
the context of one that emerges haphazardly as a result of independent growth in various areas of knowledge.

Two examples of this type of synthesis are given in War-

wick (1975), one of which is his own and the other that of the
New Zealand Post Primary Teachers' Association (1971). Warwick
starts with three basic ideas - man, environment and interaction. From these he derives eight major sub-divisions - communication, human sciences, practical work, environmental
sciences, rural science, quantitative expression, creative
studies and spiritual values. To these he adds a ninth integrative element which he calls synoptics and which is aimed at
ensuring that the central ideas of the curriculum are well represented in each sub-division and do in fact bind the whole
thing together. In addition he incorporates within the structure some important considerations about how children learn and
make use of knowledge. The New Zealand scheme is developed
from two basic ideas - empirical and non-empirical studies -
which are used to construct a curriculum consisting of five
areas:

- Investigating the Environment (sciences, geography)
- Investigating Human Behaviour (history, psychology,
  economics)
- Enquiring into Symbolic/Logical Relationships (lan-
  guages, mathematics)
- Self-expression/Communication (art, music, literature,
  physical education)
- Analytical/Reflective Studies (philosophy, sociology).

Two important features of such schemes are the novel arrangements of subject-matter and the use of subjects additional to
those traditionally taught in school.

g) *Functional Types: Intrinsic and Extrinsic*

The foregoing discussion of structural types of integration has been about organising knowledge for curriculum purposes in ways aimed at overcoming the difficulties posed by the
fragmentation of knowledge. Structural integration represents
an attempt on the part of teachers to present an integrated
view of the world to children. The fundamental problem, however, is not just that knowledge, when created, tends to become
differentiated and fragmented, but that it also tends to become dissociated from the experiences from which it was derived.
When taught, knowledge is often unaccompanied by these experiences and those who learn it in such circumstances often find
it unreal and irrelevant.

It will be noted that the move from weaker forms of structural integration, such as summation, towards stronger forms, such as holistic synthesis, has been accompanied by increasing emphasis on the need to keep knowledge grounded in experience. The move from structural to functional types may be viewed as the completion of this process. Whereas structural types represent the different ways in which the teacher can structure knowledge in order to present it in an integrated form, functional types refer to those ways in which children's learning experiences can be organised for the purpose of developing integrative ability. The shift is from a subject-centred approach to an experience-centred approach in which knowledge is used as a resource. It is important to note, however, that the two are often inseparable in practice, particularly at the functional level where some approach to knowledge, even in its differentiated form is often implied.

The distinction between intrinsic and extrinsic types originates to some extent in the difference between psychological and social forms of learning behaviour. In the one case the integrative factors focus on the individual as a learner and involve motivation and interest, in the other they relate to ways in which the individual deals with issues in the social context in which he lives.

h) Functional Types: Intrinsic Category

Consideration of the psychological principles involved in learning has led to the development of a number of different approaches to the curriculum which enable teachers to provide integrative learning experiences for children. Though these approaches are all very similar, they do arise from different aspects of learning behaviour and consequently four types can be identified. The first promotes integrative learning through needs and interests, the second through activity, the third through enquiry, and the fourth through experience.

1) Integrative Learning through Needs and Interests

One of the criticisms of the traditional, subject-centred curriculum is that it presents a very fragmented picture of reality and bears little resemblance to the world as experienced by children. The result is that many young people become disinterested in and alienated by school learning. To counteract this tendency it has been suggested that the curriculum should be based not on the nature of knowledge but on the needs and interests of children. It is argued that these should not just be used for motivational purposes but should constitute the material out of which the curriculum can be developed. One justification for this approach is the claim that it leads to the child discovering how to differentiate his own experience and in the end has the advantages of both disciplined and highly motivated learning.

Many of the ways in which this has been tried have involved forms of integration. The idea of a centre of interest, for example, combines the motivating power of interest with the possibility of extending the interest into appropriate fields of knowledge. Topic work, as Hubbard and Salt (1970) rightly point out, has similar potential. But perhaps the best known way of enabling young children to develop their own cognitive structures on a needs and interest basis is what is popularly known as 'the integrated day' (Brown and Precious, 1968; Taylor, 1971; Walton, 1971). It is also a method that involves activity, enquiry and experience, but because its foundation lies in the needs and interests of young children, it will be described more fully here than in the other sections. Generally speaking it fulfils two main purposes. It allows the natural flow of learning activities to proceed without the interruption of a timetable and it provides for simultaneous development of different aspects of growth and learning. This is achieved by spatial organisation of the classroom on an interest area basis which, in effect, replaces the timetable and allows the children to move freely from one activity to another, drawing on different subject areas as they do so. Thus one part of the classroom may be a science area, another an art area, another a reading area, and so on. Social, intellectual, emotional, physical and aesthetic growth can take place at rates suited to the development of each child, and language and thought, activity and creativity, work and play can advance in relation to each other. The integrated day, however, is no panacea. It can have disastrous consequences for the educational development of children if placed in the hands of an insensitive, inexperienced and misinformed teacher who mistakenly believes that the freedom which the children enjoy stems from an unstructured, and therefore unplanned, educational environment. The need for structure and the demands on the teacher in terms of planning, preparation and recording are just as great in the integrated day as they are in more formal methods of teaching.

As far as lifelong learning is concerned such approaches, as well as some of those presently to be described, have consid-

erable significance. In the first place they make a very obvious contribution to the education of the total man, being concerned with the integrity of the person and not just with the
unity of knowledge. Secondly they provide educational situations in which children become, to some extent, responsible for
their own learning. They learn the techniques of learning as
well as the content of knowledge. And thirdly, schemes such as
the integrated day help to preserve the unity of learning by
holding together in a coherent educational environment those
aspects of learning, such as thought and action, work and play,
that tend to become dichotomised in later schooling.

2) Integrative Learning through Activity

The activity approach to learning rests on the assertion
that learners are not just passive recipients of knowledge but
are actively engaged in the continual reconstruction of their
cognitive fields. Learning is part of doing and doing is conducive to learning. Learning is not a part of living but a
feature of it. Knowledge is thus viewed instrumentally and is
best obtained in the practical situations to which it is related.

It is hardly necessary to point out to teachers that the
most famous of all activity methods is the project, advocated
by Kilpatrick and Dewey. Apart from being an approach which
allows for the integration of subject matters in real-life
situations, it is one which ensures the alignment of learning
in school and learning in the wider world outside. It therefore helps to provide a continuity of learning in all phases
of life and in so doing is conducive to lifelong education.

3) Integrative Learning through Enquiry

Heuristic, discovery or enquiry methods exploit the natural curiosity of children, which is often dampened by didactic
teaching, and employ modes of understanding and ways of knowing
characteristic of certain forms of experience. Heurism is essential to science, close to creativity in the arts, and in
personal terms associated with a sense of identity.

In contrast to receptive learning, discovery learning is
a dynamic cognitive process in which the structure of knowledge
is not received ready-made from the teacher but is progressively
created by the pupil himself. By developing an approach to
learning which is active and creative, and which produces fresh

insights and new learning when applied in different situations, he is acquiring a skill which will stand him in good stead long after he has left school. He will be more likely to be able to solve problems for himself in the future than to reiterate other people's solutions for their problems in the past.

One significant attempt to introduce enquiry learning on an interdisciplinary basis as a planned part of the educational programme at the secondary level is that of James (1968). She introduced the idea of interdisciplinary enquiry so that pupils could use the disciplines in concert for the understanding of the world in which they live, for the solution of problems, and for the reconstitution and amplification of knowledge. In a latter publication (James, 1969) she advocated her system of interdisciplinary enquiry as a means of promoting an open approach to education and the curriculum.

4) *Integrative Learning through Experience*

Knowledge is second-hand experience; life is always first-hand experience. The teacher's task is, wherever possible to bridge this gap between idea and actuality. This can be done in several ways. It can be done to some extent through the child-centered curriculum, or by strengthening the links between school and community (Neagley and Evans, 1967). It can be done by involving children in practical activities rather than theoretical lessons. It can be done by using materials as well as ideas. And in many cases it can only be done by using integrated approaches rather than subject teaching, though the latter does not necessarily exclude the experimental approach.

The provision of experience-centred programmes is, however, more difficult in some areas than in others. In the area of social and interpersonal learning it is particularly difficult, as Shaver and Larkins (1973) point out, though recent developments suggest some interesting possibilities. The proposal of Wolsk (1975), for example, for an experience-centred curriculum aimed at fostering international understanding, are noteworthy.

i) *Functional Types: Extrinsic Category*

Here the change is from those types of integration which derive their purpose and function from the learning process itself, to those types which derive their significance from a

wider context. These are integrative forces with social rather
than psychological origins which, when channelled into the
school curriculum, have the effect of pulling it together and
giving it direction. They are of two kinds, inductive and deductive.

1) Inductive (Problem) Approaches

Inductive approaches are based on specific problems in
society which require interdisciplinary cooperation for their
understanding and solution. Examples of these problems are
health and safety, poverty and wealth, courtship and marriage,
home and family life, personal relationships, war and peace,
race and immigration, food and hunger, law and order, vandalism,
pollution, conservation, and so on. It is characteristic of
such issues that they are of a practical nature, of contemporary concern, and require the cooperation of all men for their
solution. They are the kind of issues that are frequently
dealt with in topic and project work and it is Kirk's (1973)
opinion that they provide one of the strongest arguments for
the validity of integrated work in schools. They certainly
form a useful rendezvous for learning and living.

2) Deductive (Teleological) Approaches

Functional integration of a deductive or teleological nature is characteristic of certain curricula dominated by some
transcendent purpose, some overarching idea, some ideology or
conviction. Such ideas give direction and purpose to many of
the educational experiences provided. While such curricula may
to some extent be internally consistent, they can sometimes be
socially disintegrative if the ideas on which they are based do
not have some universal reference.

The simplest and most obvious example of such a curriculum
was that developed in Church schools for the propagation of
Christianity, but more contemporary examples might be curricula
developed on the basis of the democratic ideal in America, or
on the communist ideal in Russia, or for the public school or
comprehensive systems in Britain, or for education for self-
reliance in Tanzania.

2.3   The Ubiquity of Types

Types of integration, like subjects and disciplines, exist

only in the minds of men. When embodied in action they lose their identities and live a kind of symbiotic existence anywhere and everywhere, and often in the most unlikely places. Action may not kill types but it ruins their autonomy! Consequently the divisions which have been drawn on paper in the preceding pages, do not really exist in the classroom for every teacher in action employs more than one of them, and often many simultaneously. What the typology may do is help the teacher identify those that he either wishes to escape from or to emulate.

CHAPTER 3

FUNCTIONS OF INTEGRATION

Each of the varieties of integration identified in the previous chapter fulfils specific functions (1). To identify varieties is in one sense to differentiate functions. Some types of integration, for example, aim to present to pupils a coherent picture of knowledge, whereas others aim to facilitate integrative learning. On that basis the functions are specific to the categories. It was also observed, however, that in reality the categories are not necessarily independent; ideally, they should be mutually reinforcing. Presentation of integrated material should encourage integrative thinking, and integrative learning experiences should contribute to the development of appropriate cognitive structures. It is doubtful, in fact, if the one can or should take place without the other.

In this chapter attention is focussed not on the specific functions of particular categories, but on the more general educational purposes served by curriculum integration. These have been grouped under three headings and described as epistemological, psychological and social. Epistemological functions are concerned with aspects of knowledge, psychological

---

[1] The terms 'function' and 'functional' as used in this and the preceding chapter may confuse some readers. The term 'functional' in Chapter 2 was used to refer to specific types of integration. It is therefore a technical term. The term 'functions' as used in this chapter is a more general term with a much wider significance. It is used to describe the uses that can be made of integration generally, whether structural or functional. As a rough guide the reader may find it helpful to regard the adjective 'functional' as referring to types, and the noun 'functions' as referring to uses.

functions with aspects of learning, and social functions with certain aspects of classroom interaction and school-community relationships.

Before discussing these, however, it is necessary to make one important point about the relationship between the respective functions of curriculum integration and subject teaching. Some of the functions to be discussed in the following pages are characteristic only of integrated teaching. For instance, the constraints of logic will permit only integrated teaching to counteract the proliferation of subjects and the fragmentation of knowledge. Other functions are not the monopoly of integration but are served by both subject and inter-subject approaches. For example, subjects as well as projects can interest children and make a significant contribution to their personality development. Such unity of purpose is in line with the views previously expressed about subjects and integration. It will be recalled that the two were not considered to be contradictory since subjects are the product of integrative processes. Even so, it is the existence of subjects that makes integration necessary, and many of these common functions are badly served by forms of teaching that are excessively subject-centred. In such cases integration probably has the edge on subject teaching. To get the functions of integration and subject teaching in perspective it is important to bear these points in mind.

3.1   Epistemological Functions

There are three ways in which curriculum integration can help the teacher in dealing with knowledge. It can help him to cope with changes in knowledge; it can help him to inter-relate different areas of knowledge; and it can help him to make sense of, and find purpose in, knowledge as a whole.

a) Coping with Changes in Knowledge

Knowledge as it exists in the mind is always changing; knowledge that is recorded in books is resistant to change. This difference between knowledge as an aspect of experience and knowledge as a record of experience is reflected in the difference between integrated and subject approaches to teaching and learning. Subject approaches tend to be book-centred; integrated approaches have the reputation of being experience-centred. It follows, therefore, that integrated teaching is more readily adaptable, more open to change than subject teaching. It can help the teacher to deal with three aspects of the changing face of knowledge: its expansion, its obsolescence and its fragmentation.

Perhaps the most striking of these changes is what is now popularly known as the knowledge explosion. In recent years knowledge has increased at such a rate that, in terms of sheer quantity, it has, from the point of view of the curriculum planner, almost become unmanageable. Decisions about what to put into and what to leave out of the curriculum are now very difficult to make, particularly on the basis of factual knowledge alone. One of the claims made for curriculum integration is that it helps teachers and pupils to deal with this quantity problem. Given the limited time available, a broader range of disciplines can be covered if the curriculum is organised around key concepts and basic principles which represent a synthesis of ideas from related fields. Efficiency and economy in learning would seem to derive much more from the understanding of such concepts and principles than from the assimilation of a multitude of often disconnected facts. Human relationships, for example, which are a central concept of history, religion, ethics, sociology, psychology and even politics and economics, can provide a focal point for the construction of an integrated programme through which the fundamentals of these subjects can be taught. One might even venture to say that the significance attached to such key concepts can be a determinant of the quality of teaching. Many subjects, even as presented in weighty academic textbooks, can become obscurred by sheer factual excrescence and much of their meaningfulness lost to the learner. Integration can provide a very useful service in returning the mind to the basic principles of the varieties of knowledge.

It also provides a similar service as far as the obsolescence of knowledge is concerned. When knowledge becomes out of date the most vulnerable aspects are not the basic cognitive structures but the factual content. At the factual level, therefore, forms of teaching which rely on cognitive infrastructures rather than upon factual superstructures are more likely to be adaptable to change. The need for constant curriculum renewal arising from the growth and obsolescence of knowledge involves a continual process of reinterpretation, the removal of outmoded material, and the incorporation of new knowledge (O.E.C.D., 1966). Integrated curricula, which lack the factual permanence and rigidity of subject curricula, are more given to this type of flexibility.

The most obvious use of integrated studies lies in their
capacity for counteracting the ever increasing fragmentation of
knowledge. There is a sense in which knowledge can only develop by becoming more specialised and this inevitably means increased differentiation and further fragmentation. There is
another sense, however, in which knowledge can only become
meaningful and useful if an understanding of the increasing
complexity of the interrelatedness of its parts accompanies
their tendency to proliferate. Integration helps to provide
this holistic perspective in a world of increasing particular-
ity. As the ally rather than the enemy of differentiation, it
can help us to see both the wood and the trees.

b) Interrelating Different Areas of Knowledge

Such changes in knowledge, and particularly those arising
from its tendency to fragment, provide some justification for
integrated approaches. Quite apart from the degree of fragmentation, however, there are inherent in the structure of
knowledge serious divisions of a permanent kind which any person aspiring to be educated must understand. These divisions
seem to persist irrespective of change though changes such as
we have mentioned aggravate them. They arise not so much from
the proliferation of subjects as from the distinctiveness of
the disciplines, though any tendency towards subject-centred
or discipline-centred teaching has the effect not only of
leaving them unexplained, but also of increasing their divisiveness. It is part of the raison d'être of integrative teaching to assist in the healing of such divisions by placing the
separate areas of knowledge in the context of a larger community of understanding.

These divisions, previously hinted, are inherent in the
nature of experience. They arise from the consciousness of
ourselves as both subject and object and from the many variations of this dichotomy which we encounter through our experience of the world. Thought and action, reason and emotion,
theory and practice, particular and general, quality and quantity, our relationship with people and our relationship with
things are but a few examples. Though such polarities become
fused in action, they tend to become separated in thought. When
embodied in the curriculum they achieve an unwarranted indepen-
dence. So we get the distinction between the humanities and
the sciences, between aesthetic and practical subjects, between
inductive and deductive approaches to knowledge, between the
moral and the technical, between the religious and the secular,

and so on.

When these are presented as separate entities in the curriculum two misconceptions arise. The first is that certain
ways of knowing or modes of experience characteristic of a discipline are thought to be the prerogative of its practitioners,
and the second, that these ways of knowing or modes of experience are thought to be conferred on the individual only through
the formality of the disciplines and not through the actuality
of experience. Thus it is often assumed, for example, that
creativity is the prerogative of the artist, objectivity the
prerogative of the scientist and that both these human characteristics are mediated only through science and art. Not only
are different types of experience isolated and compartmentalised,
but a wedge is driven between experience as the origin of knowledge and knowledge as the product of experience.

These assumptions arising from formal knowledge are quite
unwarranted. If the attitudes, ways of thinking, methods of
enquiry, and forms of behaviour characteristic of the disciplines do not exist in the realities of everyday living then
knowledge is indeed separate from life. Such a view is clearly
untenable. The way in which scientists look at the world is
not peculiar to scientists for it is simply a development of
one of the ways we all look at the world. And so it is with
the perspective of the artist, or the mathematician, or the
historian - all such perspectives are common to all. What the
disciplines do is to extend and enrich those aspects of experience which are the inheritance of all human beings, and what
integration attempts to do is to restore the unity of experience to its divided but developed representation in the curriculum.

c) *Providing a Sense of Purpose*

What has just been said about knowledge in its different
manifestations implies that where there is opposition and con-
tradiction within knowledge, it is unlikely to convey any sense
of common purpose. A curriculum which evolves as a collection
of different types of knowledge and is taught on a subject, or
even a discipline, basis is similarly divisive and a potential
source of confusion for the growing child. As he passes from
one subject to another on the time-table, he is confronted by
very different views of the world, of life and of reality. In
the hands of a skilful teacher, who is aware of such differences,
he will be helped and encouraged to evaluate these different

modes of understanding within the meaningful perspective of his own life, but where there is no such skill or comprehensiveness of viewpoint insecurity and loss of purpose can result.

The situation is aggravated by the fact that not all the subjects on the school time-table have the same status or hold the same importance for all. Some are given a larger share of the available time than others and this varies to some extent with age-range. Language, for example, occupies a significant place in the schooling of young children, but the extent of its contribution diminishes as the basic skills are acquired. History, on the other hand, plays little part in the early years of schooling but increases its influence in the middle and later years. Though such structuring of the curriculum on the basis of the developmental needs of children is important, it does not in itself help children to appreciate the validity of the differing perspective on reality provided by various types of knowledge. This means that while the functions of individual curriculum components may be clear and indeed justified, the relationship between their several purposes may never in fact have been worked out.

Integration of the curriculum is fundamentally concerned with this problem (Unesco, 1976c). It is not sufficient that each curriculum component should serve its own purpose; it is equally important that, in so doing, it should simultaneously serve some transcendent purpose which can be identified as the purpose of the curriculum as a whole. This neither implies that all curriculum components should serve the same purpose, nor that different purposes cannot be served by different curricula. But it does imply that the divergence of purpose in the various disciplines would seem to prohibit any of them being adopted as the source of the overriding purpose. As far as the disciplines are concerned, such a purpose must be both transcendent and all-inclusive, which means it should be derived from the source of the disciplines and the context in which they have significance. In the perspective of lifelong education such a source can only be the life of man himself, and the context the human situation in which he is involved. In such a setting it is the purpose of integration to ensure that the curriculum is thoroughly humanistic, that its various components produce a blend of experience conducive to a sense of humanity. In today's complex world this is a daunting task.

3.2   Psychological Functions

The psychological functions served by integrative teaching can be subdivided into those which help to make the curriculum more consistent with the conditions of learning, and those
which have a beneficial effect on other aspects of personality.

a) Providing a Curriculum Conducive to Learning

There are several ways in which integrative teaching com-
plies with the conditions of learning.

In the first place integrative teaching provides opportunity for organising curriculum material on psychological, rather
than purely logical, grounds. This is particularly the case
with those types of integration which we described as functional and which attempt to provide learning experiences based on
the needs, interests, curiosity and activity of children. But,
even in the case of some structural types, the psychological
argument holds good, for the emphasis on conceptual structure
is in line with the learning theories advanced by cognitive
psychologists such as Piaget and Bruner. The main difference
is that in the latter case the dictates of the logical structures of the disciplines are more likely to be followed than
in the former. It is the claim of psychologists such as Ausubel
(1967) that curriculum material organised on psychological,
rather than logical, principles is more conducive to effective
learning.

Secondly, teaching which is integrative has close links
with the concrete experiences and practical situations of everyday life. Pupils are not required to learn academic abstrac-
tions, but to develop their own patterns of thought through experience and exploration of an appropriate educational environment. The role of practical activity is crucial not only for
childhood learning but for the development of formal and prop-
ositional thinking in later years. In this respect, therefore,
an integrated-type curriculum would seem to have a significant
contribution to make to the formative years of a child's education (Lee, 1971).

Thirdly, it is claimed, for example by Choat (1971), that
integrative teaching is highly effective in motivating children
to learn. Whereas subject teaching depends to a considerable
extent on extrinsic forms of motivation such as examinations
and competition, integrative teaching stimulates interest by

emphasising the concrete rather than the abstract, by encour-
aging pupil involvement and participation, and by providing
opportunities for cooperative learning.

Fourthly, integrative teaching as an element in lifelong
education teaches children how to learn rather than what they
should know. The emphasis is upon the procedural rather than
the substantive elements in learning. Very often factual information that is memorised is soon forgotten, but ways of knowing that are internalised are more lasting. The emphasis here
is upon a learning process that is dynamic and not static (Owen,
1973) and one in which the pupil assumes considerable responsibility for his own learning (Meister, 1973).

Finally, two comments by Tyler (1949) would seem to be a
fitting conclusion to this list of ways in which integration
can promote learning. He maintains that effective learning
often follows frequent use of information in a variety of contexts. Integrated curricula can provide such opportunities for
the application of knowledge. And he further maintains that
while integrated learnings are likely to reinforce each other,
learnings that are inconsistent are likely to interfere with
each other.

While there is little empirical evidence to support such
claims, they do gain some validity from the logic of integration and the observations of those who have used it in their
teaching.

b) Promoting Personality Development through Learning

From a psychological point of view the next question we
must consider is whether integrative teaching has any significant contribution to make to the development of the personality.
When compared with subject teaching does it have any obvious
advantages as far as personal growth and self-actualisation
are concerned? Again this is an area in which there is very
little evidence on which to form any considered judgement, but
some reasoned arguments can be presented on the basis of what
is already known about subject-centred and integrative teaching.

It is a popularly held view that the study of certain
subjects seems to produce particular types of people. Many
people have stereotyped images of, for example, artists, scientists, historians and physical educationists, but would not
claim to know whether the subject creates the person or whether

the person, being what he is, chooses to study one subject
rather than another.

The researchers in this field would seem to have come to
a similar conclusion, though their findings shed some useful
light on the problem from the point of view of integration.
Hudson (1967, 1970) suggests that education in the arts and
the sciences may somehow be linked with certain personality
types, namely divergers and convergers respectively. Divergers
like to express their feelings but are weak at precise logical
thinking; convergers have rather limited emotional lives but
considerable intellectual freedom. While Hudson suggests with
some caution that an arts education may produce divergence, and
a science education convergence, he does add that they look
very like systems of cultural indoctrination. Other studies,
for example Musgrove (1971), would seem to support such a contention.

Apart from varying in their predispositions towards different subject areas, people would also seem to differ in the
ways in which they process and organise information in their
minds. They display different cognitive styles, different ways
of receiving information and fitting it into their own cognitive
patterns (Klein, 1970). While many of these styles are not
directly relevant to this study, a number of them would appear
to be concerned with the ability of individuals to integrate
knowledge (Cropley, 1976, 1977). People vary in the range of
experience to which they react and in the extent to which they
interpret such experience. Some are capable of a broad perspective and organise their thoughts in global terms, while
others are more restricted in their reactions and interpret
their experience from a much narrower viewpoint. Cropley (1976)
argues that the implications of this for curriculum organisation are twofold. In the first place, cognitive functioning
at a global level is more likely to develop from a unified rather than a fragmented curriculum. Secondly, since people have
different learning styles, some prefer to receive information
in a holistic way, either in a structured form or in terms of
broad principles, while others learn best from detailed information. As far as the curriculum is concerned, he concludes that
none of these approaches is ideal and that variety in presentation is therefore to be commended.

Such work raises some interesting questions as far as integration and personality are concerned. If specialist education tends to produce polarisation of personality traits, per-

haps a more balanced education of the personality could be
achieved by a greater degree of integration. If, on the other
hand, specialisation is the product of deep-seated personality
traits, the effects of integration on the personality could be
more problematic.

More confident claims can be made about these aspects
of personality development that are provided for throuyn integration compared with subject teaching. Subject teaching focuses on the intellect and neglects, or even ignores, other aspects of the personality. Richmond (1971) argues that in the
context of a subject-oriented curriculum, emotional, social,
moral and even practical considerations are reduced to insignificance by being non-examinable. Schwab (1971), in similar
vein, contends that schools tend to treat all disciplines as if
they were theoretical, thereby subscribing to a form of educational reductionism.

In contrast, many forms of integrative teaching attach
considerable importance to non-cognitive aspects of personality.
The needs and interests of children as individuals, their social,
emotional and moral development as members of a class group,
and their wide-ranging behavioural repertoire are central to
such schemes as the integrated day or a social studies project.
Concern for such a variety of personality characteristics is a
feature of many integrated approaches reported in the literature (e.g. Dyasi, 1974; Jones, 1975). Very often, however, the
constraints of the practical situation in the classroom make it
difficult to translate such ideals into actualities and even
the best-intentioned teachers revert to more traditional practices. Hamilton (1975), for example, found that aspects other
than the cognitive tended to be omitted from tests given to
children on integrated programmes.

It could also be argued that integrative teaching, with
its emphasis on self-directed learning and personal responsibility, helps to promote in children a satisfactory self-concept.
There can be little doubt that the damage done to the integrity
of children's personalities by competitive and examination-
ridden forms of traditional education can be seriously debilitating. Many integrated forms of learning require for success
not a stereotyped intellectual response, but a more rounded
form of individual achievement. Though the exercise of personal responsibility in learning is more demanding, the degree of
satisfaction to be gained is more likely to be conducive to a
sense of personal well-being.

3.3   Social Functions

Three categories of social function can be served by integrative teaching. These can be described as teaching and
learning through sharing, coping with interdisciplinary issues,
and relating school and society.

a)   Teaching and Learning through Sharing

Competition and cooperation tend to be the respective
features of subject-based and integrative teaching, and these
affect the performance of both teacher and pupil. In the past
teaching has tended to be a lonely enterprise, each teacher
working on his own unaided by and often in competition with his
colleagues. Pupils, too, have shared a similar fate. Many of
the old, school-boy virtues and vices have stemmed from this
competitive element in education - passing or failing examinations, being top or bottom of the class, copying, or being a
'swot'. Systems of rewards and punishments, such as stars for
the successful and stripes for the wayward, have also had a
competitive basis. The tragedy of such excess lies not so much
in the disadvantages gained as in the opportunities lost, for
learning is a form of sharing and it is rather pointless to expect the one to develop by prohibiting the other.

It is also ironic that while subject teaching fosters individualism through group learning, integrative teaching encourages cooperation through individualised learning. Yet,
while excessive subject teaching discourages cooperation, excessive integrative teaching does not necessarily exclude competition. Clearly, all teaching should provide opportunity for
both, but what we are particularly concerned to demonstrate in
this section is the closeness of the link between integration
and cooperation. Children learn a remarkable amount from each
other in the course of their everyday lives, and this avenue
to knowledge should not be closed to them in school. This is
one argument in favour of mixed ability teaching, a form of social integration that might well be a natural concomitant of
curriculum integration. Teachers likewise can learn a great
deal from each other, and as Hamilton (1975) has shown, the degree and effectiveness of integration depends on the extent to
which teachers can communicate and work together. Many types
of integrated work would be impossible without such cooperation.
To cross subject boundaries, teachers have to plan their work
together, assist each other in the teaching situation, and continue a working dialogue not only between themselves but also

with the children. The children for their part are often required to make their individual contributions through work in
groups, to assist each other when necessary, and to learn from
their own strengths and mistakes and those of their fellows.
Such a situation affords considerable opportunity for teaching
and learning through sharing.

b) Coping with Interdisciplinary Issues

It has already been observed (on pages 40-41) that one of
the varieties of curriculum integration involves dealing with
issues in contemporary society that can be fully understood
only through an interdisciplinary approach. Integration has a
very significant part to play in the education of children and
adults by introducing them to such issues. Without repeating
what was said previously, it can be affirmed that the kind of
contribution that integration can make in this respect is a
very positive one, for the issues are generally of a practical
nature and of direct concern to the children themselves. If
not dealt with through some form of integration, they would at
best be misunderstood or at worst never dealt with at all. Sex
education is perhaps one of the best examples. It is a subject
that can only be taught adequately through many different subjects on the school curriculum and through the use of subjects
such as psychology and sociology which are not normally taught
in school. The use of some form of integration is the only way
in which this can be done.

c) Relating School and Society

One of the inevitable consequences of educational involvement in contemporary social issues is the forging of closer
links between school and society. The pursuit of a purely academic approach to learning often has the effect of dissociating
knowledge from the real situations of life. Subjects tend to
get bound up in their own traditions and are often not amenable
to the kind of transformations that are necessary for meaningful learning in today's world. Knowledge in school thus becomes dissociated from knowledge in society. It is for such
reasons that sociologists such as Bernstein (1971) differentiate
between the 'commonsense knowledge' of the everyday world and
the 'uncommonsense knowledge' of the school. In these terms
schooling becomes a form of socialisation out of the sphere of
the family and peer group and into the world of the scholar.
Many teachers who have had an academic education, have the op-
posite kind of experience when they start teaching, particularly

when they have to deal with integrated topics. They find that, despite their academic education, they have to learn topics even in their own subject areas which are relatively new to them, but which are only of marginal interest to academics (Blyth et al., 1975). Examples of such topics are transport, costume, the weather, and details of farming or forestry.

The role of integration in such activities is quite clear. It has an inbuilt facility for merging school and society and making the concerns of the one the concern of the other.

3.4   Types and Functions

As a conclusion to this chapter it is necessary to consider the relationship between types and functions of integration. Since there are many types and many functions, it is obvious that each type cannot fulfil every function. Even if this were possible, such correspondence would be no guarantee that the practice of a particular type in the classroom would inevitably achieve the functions as stated. The teaching-learning situation is of such complexity that predictions are seldom accurate. It would be rash to claim that any particular type would necessarily accomplish even a limited number of tasks. In any case, some functions are more difficult to fulfil than others and for this reason also any general forecast of what might be achieved is likely to be misleading.

Despite this caveat, however, there are two features of the relationship between types and functions that are significant. The first is that there is quite a close correspondence between types and functions, as was suggested at the beginning of the chapter. Structural forms of integration, concerned for the most part with the organisation of knowledge, make their strongest contribution in the epistemological field. Functional types, on the other hand, are more suited to the achievement of psychological and social objectives. It will be recalled that this latter distinction provided the basis for differentiating between intrinsic and extrinsic functional types. Take, for example, two teachers, one of history and the other of geography, who devise a combined programme on a block basis. In so doing they are obviously relating different areas of knowledge, even if only in a limited way; they are conceivably attempting to achieve a purpose that transcends the purposes of their individual disciplines; and it is possible that they may be attempting to adapt the content of their subjects to fit

recent developments in knowledge. Such a programme may achieve
some of the psychological and social functions that have been
discussed but this will depend more on how the teachers implement the programme than on the programme as such. In the case
of a primary school teacher, however, who plans to undertake a
project on water with her class, the psychological and social
functions are more intrinsic to the programme than they are in
the previous example, though their operation will, of course,
again depend on the social structure of the classroom. Nevertheless, a project does serve certain epistemological functions
as well, and such comprehensiveness of purpose on the part of
functional types is the second significant feature of the relationship between types and functions.

There would appear to be a hierarchical relationship between the types as listed in the typology, particularly as far
as functions are concerned. It is likely that a teacher who
deals with a contemporary problem such as pollution will adopt a
project approach, employ some form of heuristic or activity method, provide for individual interests, and use small group teaching methods and a broad range of disciplines. Many of the functions listed will therefore have been fulfilled in one way or
another. On the other hand such a broad range of functions is
less likely to characterise an integrated programme of the summative type which is little better than collaborative subject
teaching. It would appear, therefore, that in general terms
and everything else being equal, a broader range of functions
is served by those types of integration at the functional level
than by those at the structural level of the typology.

Whatever else this analysis reveals, it indicates quite
clearly that curriculum integration is not a uniform activity
which always achieves the same results. There are many shades
of curriculum integration and a variety of purposes served by
them. It is important, therefore, that the teacher should be
able to choose wisely from the range of possibilities available
so that the particular purposes that he has in mind can have the
greatest chance of being fulfilled. This matter of choice is
an important feature of curriculum planning which is one of the
topics discussed in the next chapter.

CHAPTER 4

TEACHING STYLES AND
INTEGRATED APPROACHES

In this chapter the ways in which curriculum integration affects methods of teaching will be examined. This will include consideration of the planning, implementation and assessment of integrated work, but to set the stage for such discussion it is necessary to consider the relationship between integrated approaches and progressive methods of teaching.

4.1   Are Integrated Approaches Necessarily Progressive?

A recent survey of educational literature and teachers' views on progressive and traditional educational practices (Bennett, 1976) indicates very clearly that many educationists associate progressive education with the integration of subject matter and traditional forms of teaching with separate subject provision. In this view integration is an accompaniment of the progressive movement in education along with child-centred teaching and experience-centred learning. In such a context integrated approaches could only be progressive.

An implication of this view is that integration can occur only in a progressive environment and in the absence of separate subject teaching. This is clearly not so. It not only implies a very restricted view of the integrative process in education, but it does not fit the facts. Many integrated forms of teach-

---

[1] The word 'style' has been used in this context because it is wider than 'method' or 'procedure' and includes the element of personal interpretation and the particular mode of implementation that makes all educational activities idiosyncratic.

ing occur within a subject-based curriculum and are taught by subject specialists (Mitchell, Hogan and West, 1972).

The question being asked in this section, however, is not whether integration is a characteristic of progressivism but whether the practices necessary for integration are inevitably of a progressive kind. Again there is a school of thought which seems to think that they are. Stenhouse (1968), for example, sees the integrative teacher as an adviser rather than an instructor. In the type of humanities programme with which he was involved such a role could well be appropriate, but it would be unwise to infer from this that all integrative teaching should follow such a stereotyped pattern.

The need for caution arises from the typology developed in Chapter 2. There a very broad range of types of integration was identified and an equally broad range of methods is necessary for their implementation. At the one extreme, a combined course to which different subject specialists made their own individual contributions could well be taught in a formal manner, but this would not exclude the possibility of any particular contributor employing more modern methods if he so wished. Neither subject nor integrated teaching has exclusive rights to formality or informality. At the other extreme, a programme organised on the basis of an integrated day is more likely to be conducted in the progressive tradition, though it could well include a reasonable amount of what would be considered quite formal teaching. At the risk of generalising, one might conclude that functional types of integration are more likely to incorporate progressive methods of teaching than structural types, which, because of their subject emphasis, encourage more formal approaches. But this kind of statement is but an indication of likely tendencies, not a blue-print for action. In the practical situation and with respect for his pupils, the teacher must use whatever method, be it progressive or traditional, that maximises learning. Practical reason rather than emotional fervour should determine his course of action.

4.2   Planning an Integrated Programme

a) *The Importance of Planning*

The way teachers plan their work is as important an element of style as the way they behave in the classroom. In the past, consideration of teaching methods has tended to neglect the

planning process and more recent curriculum analyses have given
insufficient attention to the methodology of teaching. It ap-
pears that once the focus is upon one area of education, a tendency develops to neglect others. As far as integration is concerned planning is of paramount importance, for in integrate
teaching neither content nor method are predetermined as they
often are in subject teaching. These aspects of integrative
teaching are often strongly influenced by circumstance and this
necessitates firm decision-making on the part of the teacher
before the implementation of the programme.

Another factor that makes planning important is the number
of people that can often be involved, either directly or in-
directly, in integrated work. These can include teaching colleagues, the headmaster, children and their parents, and individuals and agencies outside the school. Bolam (1972) rightly
stresses the importance of full consultation with all such interested parties at the planning stage. Such involvement and
participation is part of the integrative process.

Furthermore integrated work often has a practical orientation. It involves concrete experiences, practical activities,
and the use of materials and resources. Unless such provision
is incorporated in the planning process, the outcome is likely
to be little more than a reversion to the teaching of theory.

Finally, there is much sense in Lawton's (1969) sugges-
tion that a curriculum is integrated only insofar as it is planned as a unity. This neither implies uniformity of content nor
of procedure but it does presuppose a unity of intention.
Achieving such consensus for action amidst diversity of viewpoint is perhaps the most difficult part of all integrated work.
If it does not characterise the planning it is unlikely to feature in the implementation.

   b) Planning Criteria

Because of the many different ways of integrating knowledge and experience, it is not possible in a study of this size
to itemize the various criteria appropriate on each case. The
criteria necessary for the successful planning of a project
would differ significantly from those relevant to the reconstruction of a whole school curriculum. It is however important that staff should be aware of the principal factors that
need to be considered in planning a programme. These are related to the characteristics of the children, to aspects of

their learning activities and to the practicalities of the
teaching situation.

As far as the children are concerned any programme of
work should suit their age and ability ranges and be of interest and use to them. It is particularly important for integrated programmes to incorporate different types of activities
related to a broad band of knowledge, and to allow for the
development of different aspects of the personality.

It should also provide for continuity in learning by being related to work covered both before and after the programme.
Horizontal relationship with subject areas is also important,
as is the need for children to develop their disciplinary understanding through integrated work.

Practical aspects also need careful consideration and
these range from time-table feasibility to adequacy of available resources. Staff cooperation and material requirements
are both necessary.

   c) *Formulating Intentions*

Teachers who rely on the factual composition of subject
matter as the basis of their intentions, or teachers who mistakenly believe that the child should choose and construct his
own curriculum have less opportunity for choice and less need
for decision-making in the planning of curricula than teachers
who wish to plan a reasonably well integrated programme. There
are several reasons for this.

In the first place the principle that integrated work
should be built on the conceptual base rather than the factual
structure of the disciplines allows for considerable choice of
both subject matter and method. The responsibility for such
choice rests with the teacher who alone can make such decisions
in the light of his personal and professional knowledge of the
pupils and the school in which he works. The variables on
which decisions are made in such a situation are not only more
numerous but also less tangible in purely teaching terms than
those underlying a strictly subject approach.

Secondly, since integration is concerned with the deep
structures of the disciplines quite early in the learning process, the teacher must provide for the use of and for practice
in high level intellectual skills in the upper reaches of

Bloom's (1956) cognitive taxonomy. This again necessitates preparation of a teaching pattern and organisational structure that are unlikely to conform to those that are characteristic of pre-packaged curriculum materials.

Thirdly, the behavioural repertoire included in integrated work is quite extensive and includes a considerable number of attitudinal and psychomotor behaviours such as are analysed in Krathwohl's (1964) and Simpson's (1966-7) taxonomies. Provision for these includes a complexity of factors of an organisational, managerial and interpersonal kind.

As part of the planning process, therefore, teachers must learn to formulate their intentions and design their curricula in ways that will ensure educational validity and operational effectiveness. The focus in planning integrated work is not on content to be covered but on behaviours to be developed, and an assessment of the value of possible educational outcomes should be an inherent part of the design.

Such a general principle, however, cannot be rigidly applied in the same way and to the same extent in every circumstance. The relationship between content as design input and behaviour as a characteristic and outcome of the educational process, will vary considerably across the broad range of possibilities extending from purely summative forms of structural integration on the one hand to experience-centred, functional curricula on the other. The nature of the content and of the behaviour are also influential, and a less rigorous application of the general principle may be appropriate in certain areas such as the humanities (Stenhouse, 1970). Furthermore, sufficient flexibility is necessary to allow for compatibility of teacher intended outcomes and children's creative responses (Eisner et al., 1969). Opportunity for the latter is also an important characteristic of integrated work and should be given adequate consideration at the planning stage.

4.3   Teaching an Integrated Programme

a) Principles of Integrative Learning

Having noted that certain types of teaching and learning are characteristic of, but not necessarily exclusive to the practice of integration, it is now necessary to examine the principles of learning and teaching that are specifically in-

volved. The first task is to discuss children's learning and
this will be done under three headings: learning to know, learning to do, and learning to be.

1) Learning to Know

An increase in children's knowledge and understanding is
a primary aim of integrated teaching. In this respect both
subject teaching and integrated teaching share the same purpose.
Their respective contributions to the educational development
of children are in fact complementary. Knowledge derived from
the integration of subjects is as significant a part of human
knowledge as the subjects themselves. This is understandable
in view of the claim that integration is an extension of, rather than a departure from, subject teaching. It is also partly
substantiated by Hirst's (1974) concept of fields of knowledge
and by Bernstein's (1971) notion of commonsense knowledge.
Learning to know thus involves learning beyond subjects and disciplines as well as through them, and much of this transcendent
learning involves integration.

A corollary of this concept of transcendent learning is
that the disciplines of knowledge should not constrain the interests and learning activities of the child. Such restriction
is educationally dysfunctional and can be minimised by the use
of integrated approaches. Children should have opportunity to
follow up their interests between subjects as well as within
subjects and such opportunity is available to them in the context of an integrated day or through the interdisciplinary activities of project work.

Furthermore, teaching which is prescriptive and expository
tends to produce circumscribed and non-adaptive forms of cognitive behaviour, whereas learning that is practical and expe-
riental tends to promote creative and productive thinking. Because subjects are closed systems, subject teaching tends to be
didactic; but because integrated activities are relatively
open, integrated teaching tends to be heuristic. In the one
children are required to accept actuality, in the other they
can probe possibility. Integrated teaching tends to encourage
individuality and freedom of choice in learning. Creativity,
learning by discovery, choice and individuality, while by no
means the monopoly of integrated teaching, have a natural affinity with it.

Implied in learning to know is learning how to know. A

Unesco (1976c) report on the content of education in the context of lifelong education suggests that curriculum content can
be chosen on the basis of four theories: encyclopaedism, which
stresses memory; formalism, which stresses intellectual apti-
tude; utilitarianism, which stresses practical activities; and
functional materialism, which combines knowledge with its functions in the theoretical and practical operations of people.
It is this functional aspect that is an important ingredient of
integrated teaching. In learning science, for example, children have to be taught to think like scientists and not just to
learn what scientists have thought (Hall, 1973). This involves
fusion of the structural and functional aspects of knowledge
and their embodiment and transformation in the thought and the
lives of people.

2) Learning to Do

Knowing is not the only goal of education. Action as well
as thought is fundamental to living, and their reciprocity is a
prerequisite of lifelong learning. From an educational point
of view this means two things: firstly, that knowledge should
be useful, and secondly, that the learning of such useful knowledge should be active learning, or what is popularly known as
learning by doing. The interdependence of these two has not
always been recognised in the past. The application of so-called
activity methods to purely theoretical knowledge of little significance for children is as spurious as it is ineffective. In
the context of integrative activities, it often means copying
from books instead of listening to teacher.

The idea that education should be useful is well established (Whithead, 1932); the idea that knowledge should be useful has not had the impact on the curricula of schools that it
might have had. Despite the phenomenal development in practical
skills, the academic myth that subject matter is enriching but
skill unrewarding still persists, even in the progressive circles of primary education. The idea of knowledge for its own
sake, which implies that it is intrinsically valuable, is a
sophisticated notion which, while not unrelated to the idea of
learning how to learn, is not one to be applied too rigorosly
in the tender years of schooling. Of all the knowledge that
could be taught, only that which is relevant and useful should
be taught. Part of the strength of integrated teaching lies in
its being able frequently to fulfil these two criteria.

Knowledge that is useful is best learned by using it.

This is the basis of learning by doing. Thus, as long ago as 1931, the Hadow Report on Primary Education in England suggested that the curriculum of the primary school should be thought of 'in terms of activity and experience rather than knowledge to be stored or facts known'. Since that time the work of Piaget in particular has confirmed the wisdom of such counsel. The point is that while useful knowledge can improve practice, practical learning can help to develop theoretical understanding. Such practical learning, as we have seen, is central to many forms of integrated work.

3) Learning to Be

Learning to be subsumes and encompasses both learning to know and learning to do. Learning is for living and not just for knowing or doing. Being is what matters to people; knowing and doing only have significance in an ontological context. Thus people who are educated are not just knowers or doers, performers of intellectual or manipulative feats. They are people with a particular quality of life, who display understanding, sensitivity and concern in their relationship to the external world and particularly to their fellow humans in it. They are those who enrich the lives of others by having learned how to enrich their own. This is why many people who do not know much, or who are not able to do a great deal, are often well educated; and it is also why some people with considerable knowledge and expertise remain uneducated. Quality of life, not quantity of knowledge, is the mark of the educated man.

Learning to be thus presupposes a particular quality of educational milieu in which the many different personal attributes of children may be nurtured. It means that opportunities should be provided through the social context and curriculum provision of the classroom for physical, emotional, social, moral as well as intellectual development. It involves the cultivation of idiosyncrasy within the framework of culture and community (Benjamin, 1949). It implies the provision of learning opportunities that will create and maintain the integrity of the personality.

The concept highlights the gap between the goals of schooling and the goals of education. The one set is scholastic, the other more broadly related to the purposes and practicalities of life. Previous discussion has highlighted the fact that integrated curricula characteristically deal with aspects of personal knowledge and issues of social concern that escape the

conceptual net of the disciplines; and they do so in ways conducive to the growth of a rounded personality and the development of a sense of social responsibility. They promote, in
other words, the principle of learning to be.

b) *The Practice of Integrative Teaching*

These principles of integrative learning have implications for the practice of teaching. Teaching that is integrative must be creative, facilitative and cooperative.

1) *Creative Teaching*

All teachers can, of course, teach creatively whether concerned with subject or integrated teaching. Creativity knows
no bounds! There are, however, two aspects of integrated teaching that imply a greater degree of resourcefulness and initia-
tive than would normally be expected in teaching which conformed
to some previously determined pattern or structure.

In the first place the teacher of an integrated programme
often has not only to create much of the material himself, but
has also to arrange the learning environment of the classroom
in such a way that integration will occur. This involves decisions relating to selection of appropriate topics and materials,
the range of knowledge to be covered, continuity with other aspects of the children's educational programme, combination of
teaching methods to be used, coordination of staff contributions, opportunities for practical application, arrangements
for use of out-of-school facilities, and the ways in which
achievement can be evaluated and progress recorded. Ability to
plan, ability to choose, and ability to decide, though by no
means unnecessary in subject teaching, are all at a premium in
integrated teaching.

Secondly, many teaching situations involving integration
are often more open-ended than those normally found in formal
classrooms, and greater spontaneity of response is involved
both on the part of the teacher and the pupils. The teacher is
no longer in control of the knowledge covered, the information
provided, the questions asked or the issues raised, and consequently his role changes from that of an authority to that of a
participant. He may be asked questions, for example, to which
he does not know the answer, and his job will be to enable the
children to find out the answers for themselves. Because the
teacher in such a situation is more vulnerable, he needs to be

more resourceful (Sutton, 1975).

2) Facilitative Teaching

The basic meaning of the word 'to teach' is to display, so that teaching is essentially the showing off of one's knowledge. The focus in teaching is upon the imparting of knowledge, and though this implies the development of understanding, teaching at this formal level involves only minimal concern for the performance of the pupil. As Milton (1973) observes, teaching emphasises what the instructor does, not what the pupil must do. The primary determinant in this interpretation of teaching is the nature of the subject matter to be taught, not the conditions necessary for learning it.

Few today would accept this one-sided view of teaching because it portrays teaching as didactic, theoretical and egocentric, the teacher being active, but the learner passive. It is the teacher's task not just to impart information but to cause pupils to learn. He is as much the facilitator of learning as he is the transmitter of knowledge.

It is in this role as facilitator of learning that the teacher is required to function in many integrated programmes. He is not just there to teach but to provide an environment of learning in which his pupils have opportunity to learn, and, to learn, if they can, more than he has to teach them. Facilitative teaching is a way of making it possible for pupils not only to learn beyond subjects but to learn beyond the limitations of the teacher's own knowledge of subjects.

3) Cooperative Teaching

Integrated teaching requires cooperation between the teacher and all those involved in his teaching - his pupils, his colleagues, parents, and others concerned with education in the community. Without such cooperation integrated teaching would not be possible, for cooperation is the social reflection of the pedagogical process.

In the classroom this takes the form of changed relationships between teacher and taught. Oeser (1960) demonstrates very clearly how the introduction of topic work brings about a change in the organisation of the classroom as a social group. From being the dominant figure in front of the class, the teacher becomes a participator in the work of a group, acting as a friendly but experienced adviser.

Professional relationships with colleagues are also affected, particularly if they were hitherto subject-based. The
validity of teaching and learning criteria derived from subjects other than one's specialism has to be recognised, content
and procedures previously predetermined have to be negotiated,
and the insulation and protection of the separate subject classroom are removed. Some teachers find such experiences difficult to cope with and they need to be very gently introduced to
the team teaching involved in integration.

Cooperation with parents is also important particularly
if integrated work is being introduced into the school for the
first time. It may even be advisable to meet parents to explain the rationale of integration or to outline any projects
envisaged. Parents can sometimes be very helpful in obtaining
the practical facilities in the locality that are often necessary for integrated work. Otherwise contacts with educational
agencies such as libraries, museums, business and industrial
concerns, have to be established.

4.4   Assessment and Evaluation of Integrated Work

The assessment of pupils and the evaluation of programmes
raise a number of important issues in the practice of curriculum
integration.

a)   Assessment of Pupils

The assessment of pupil progress in integrated programmes
is especially difficult for a number of reasons. In the first
place the criteria of success are often either more diffuse or
more difficult to trace and identify in the short term than
those for subject teaching. This varies, however, according
to type of approach and the extent to which aims and objectives
have been adequately formulated. Secondly, the extensive nature of integrated objectives, covering, as they do, so many
different aspects of personality, create particular difficulties.
In assessing personal qualities the teacher is torn between being either subjective in his judgement, or reductionist in his
procedures, that is by requiring that all responses be convert-
ed to cognitive responses. Thirdly, the tendency for work to
be undertaken in small groups makes it difficult to detect and
evaluate individual contributions. Fourthly, the span of pro-

gress is not easily identifiable and not easily placed within the continuity of the contributory disciplines. Fifthly, choice and variety of possible outcomes are much more extensive in the case of integrated teaching than in the case of subject teaching. Sixthly, consensus of contributing staff on appropriate measures is not always easy to obtain. And seventhly, the heterogeneity of integrated approaches makes any standardisation of assessment procedures difficult.

The outlook, however, is not quite as bleak as the above paragraph might suggest. There are several ways of overcoming some of these difficulties. In the first place the use of forms of continuous assessment would seem to be appropriate and this could include conventional testing procedures as well as the assessment of individual work. Secondly, the practical emphasis in much integrated work would suggest that practical expertise as well as theoretical understanding should be evaluated, and this might be done using workshop procedures, laboratory practices, simulation methods or situation-type testing according to the circumstances involved. Thirdly, at the national level, the use of examination procedures such as the Mode 3 examination for the Certificate of Secondary Education in England could be recommended. In this type of examination responsibility for the examination is placed very largely on the teachers in the school, the examining board acting as the guardian of standards and as an advisory body. This ensures uniformity of standard but allows for flexibility of procedure.

Perhaps the most important feature of assessment of integrated work, however, is that which arises from its personalised emphasis. The tendency in formal assessment procedures is to make them norm-referenced, that is to use the assessment for comparing the performance of each child with that of its peers so that a rank order of achievement can be obtained. The alternative is to use criterion-referenced measures whereby the child can assess his own progress towards the achievement of specifiable goals and use such assessment for purposes of self-improvement (Unesco, 1976a). Norm-referenced assessment is used largely for social engineering and is humiliating and debilitating. Criterion-referenced assessment is non-threatening and self-enhancing and should be used wherever possible in integrated work.

All these issues make it vitally important that accurate records of children's progress are kept and used for the furtherance of their educational development. This again has its

difficulties. In the case of an integrated day programme, for
example, a teacher may find it difficult to keep a constant
check on a class of thirty children involved in a variety of
activities. Or in the case of an interdisciplinary programme,
the involvement of a number of teachers may cause continuity
problems. Even so, a determined effort needs to be made in
each circumstance to surmount these barriers so that adequate
records of progress are kept.

   b) *Evaluation of Programmes*

   The progress of individual pupils is one indicator of the
effectiveness of a programme. In addition, however, the teacher needs to be able to judge whether or not a particular programme has been satisfactory, and what particular aspects of it
could be improved. This calls for a certain measure of self-
evaluation (Simpson, 1966) but it can also involve the adoption
of particular evaluation techniques, a number of which have
been developed in recent years. Mayer and Richmond (1975), for
example, review some of the many different instruments available
for the evaluation of integrated science teaching, and the growing number of reports on integrated work in general give considerable guidance on the sort of issues that teachers should be
particularly aware of (e.g. Schools Council, 1972; Hamilton,
1973).

4.5   Types, Functions and Styles

   The view adopted in this study that integration is an extension of rather than a substitute for subject teaching has
important implications as far as teaching styles appropriate to
the various types and functions of integration are concerned.
In general terms structural and functional types of integration
tend to be characterised by formal and informal styles of teaching respectively. A similar link was established between structural and functional types and the various functions identified
in Chapter 2. Structural types, being subject based probably
render their greatest service in the epistemological field,
whereas functional types, being experience based, are more given
to psychological and social purposes. It follows, therefore,
that while structural types tend to use formal styles to achieve
largely epistemological purposes, functional types tend to use
informal styles to achieve largely psychological and social purposes.

All this is true at a crude theoretical level, but if left unqualified, it would exemplify the mind's tendency to deceive. This is evident in a number of ways. In the first place, such an analysis assumes that the typological categories (as well as the various functions and styles) are discrete, a point that was categorically denied in Chapter 2, particularly in the paragraph on the ubiquity of types. Secondly, such mental separation polarizes subject and integrated teaching and this not only overemphasises their differences but obscures their similarities. Thirdly, such categorisation ignores the hierarchical nature of the relationship between the various types and between types and functions as described in Chapter 3. And fourthly, such cognitive reflections of reality tend to have more clearly defined boundaries than the actualities they represent. Practice, as distinct from theory, is much more conducive to the coalescence of contradictions.

In the practical situation of the classroom, therefore, there is likely to be much greater interplay between the various types, functions and styles. A comprehensive view of integration which links it with, rather than dissociates it from, subject teaching must provide for a comprehensive range of pedagogical possibilities. It is only when integration is contracted with subject teaching that it becomes associated in people's minds with extremist educational practices. When viewed as an extension of subject teaching it operates as a mediating influence between the extremes of traditionalism and progressivism and of behaviourism and romanticism for it embraces practices that in each case provides the best of both worlds. Thus integrated teaching is of such variety that it must involve the use of a comprehensive range of teaching techniques comprising both well-proven traditional methods and appropriate modern developments.

CHAPTER 5

INTEGRATION AND SCHOOL ORGANISATION

The previous chapter dealt with the influence of integration on teaching styles, on the approaches to teaching and learning employed by teachers in their interaction with children in the classroom. This chapter widens the perspective and considers the effects of integration on the school as a whole and in particular on the way in which it is organised.

The effects of many types of integration can, of course, be contained within the classroom. A teacher in a primary school wishing to do topic work need not involve either the headmaster or other colleagues except, perhaps, in a consultative or advisory capacity. But in many cases of integration this is not so. A headmaster of a middle or secondary school who wishes to introduce some form of integrated studies into his curriculum has to face serious management and administrative problems which affect the organisational structure of the school. It is these problems that are the concern of this chapter.

5.1 Integration and Social Change

a) School and Society

Schools are a form of social institution and do not exist in isolation from the rest of society. They exist in a reciprocal relationship with society, since each exerts an influence on the other. What happens in school is often a reflection of what happens outside it.

It has been suggested that the move towards integration of the curriculum is not an isolated development but a reflection of changes taking place in society generally (Bernstein,

71

1967; 1971). Bernstein argues that society is becoming more open in that the boundaries of the divisions within it are becoming more blurred. This change from a society in which individuals found security by belonging to particular groups, is characterised by a growth of individualism, an increase in pluralism, the emergence of meritocracy, and, in Durkheim's terminology, a shift from mechanical to organic solidarity. Social coherence no longer stems from the existence of large groups which share common belief systems and require their members to behave in particular ways, but from a much more complex interdependence of particular types of social function. Such changes are mirrored in school in the shift from a subject-based to an integrated curriculum.

b) Contrasting Forms of Curricular Organisation

Bernstein uses the term 'code' to refer to the basic principles which underly curriculum organisation. He distinguishes between two different types of code, a collection code and an integrated code. A collection code refers to a subject-based form of curriculum organisation, an integrated code to an integrated curriculum.

A curriculum of the collection type consists simply of a collection of subjects, each of which is separate from the other. The strength and definition of the boundaries between them indicate how well they have been categorised or classified. Strongly classified subjects stand in a closed relationship to each other. A related variable is the amount of control that the teacher has over the teaching of the subject, and this tends to be in inverse proportion to the amount of choice that the pupil has in learning it. Bernstein uses the term 'frame' to refer to the exercise of such control and choice.

Collection codes are thus characterised by strong classification and strong framing. The subjects of which they are composed are well insulated from each other and well guarded by their respective adherents. Viewed in this way, subjects are not so much cognitive reflections of reality as social institutions (Nisbet, 1957), exercising control over their membership and commanding loyalty. Their particular brand of knowledge is their private property. Entry to its mysteries is hierarchically controlled so that the ultimate truth of a subject is available only to those who have stayed the course and earned the respect of their teachers over a long period of time. To distance knowledge in this way has the effect of separating it from the realities of everyday life (Apple, 1972).

The distinguishing features of integrated curricula are in contrast to those of collection curricula. Integration results in weak classification and often weak framing. Subjects stand in a more open relationship to each other and their boundaries become blurred. The exercise of control by the teacher is more variable, however, since it depends on the nature of the relationship he establishes with his pupils. The essence of integration for Bernstein lies in the subordination of subjects to some transcendent, relational idea. In this context knowledge ceases to be a possession of the few and becomes used by all for social purposes. Teachers are more inclined to raise problems than provide solutions and pupils can exercise greater freedom of choice and autonomy. Knowledge is kept close to the everyday realities of life and the movement of learning is from the deep structures or basic principles of a subject to the more factual content on the surface. Pedagogy is based on an instrumental view of knowledge, an individualised and small group approach to learning, and greater homogeneity in the practice of teaching.

Bernstein's theory is a plausible one. Integration looks very like the pedagogical reflection of the open society, and judging from the nature of integration one might expect such an interrelationship. But to view integration as largely a uniform concept to be understood only in terms of social process, is to oversimplify it. The origins and ramifications of integration lie beyond the boundaries of sociology! But its social implications cannot be ignored and these are our present concern.

Bernstein distinguishes between two types of integrated curricula, what he calls teacher-based and teachers-based curricula. In the former, to be found mainly in infant and primary schools, one teacher is responsible for the whole curriculum; by the use of a flexible time-table and appropriate methods, he blurs the boundaries between subjects and attempts to provide a coherent educational experience. Integration involving more than one teacher is more difficult to implement, since it involves the cooperation of adherents of different subjects or disciplines. In management terms the former involves only the classroom, the latter often the whole school.

5.2   Integration and Management in the School Setting

a) *Integration and Classroom Management*

Management in the formal classroom is largely stereotyped.
The teacher has his desk, the children theirs. What the children do is for the most part determined by what the teacher
does. If he is speaking, they are listening; if he is not
speaking, they are likely to be working. Movement is similarly
determined; either they go to him, or he goes to them. So with
materials and behaviours. Except in obvious subjects like art
and physical education, paper and pencil will be prominent as
will reading and writing. Routine and regularity provide the
order of the day.

In many integrated classrooms this rather rigid management
pattern changes dramatically, though such changes are also to be
found in some progressive classrooms where the teaching remains
subject-based. We have already seen how integration affects the
relationship between teacher and pupils (page 66). A less formal and more personalised relationship develops and the teacher
has to change quite radically the ways in which he controls and
directs the class and the individuals in it.

Perhaps the most distinctive feature of the change is the
variety that is introduced into the classroom through integration. The ways in which the children are grouped for working
will vary considerably. On one occasion they may be taught as
a class, or as a whole year group with other classes; on another
they may require individual attention or small group instruction.
The range of methods and resources used for teaching is also
likely to be extensive and this affects the kind of material
and interpersonal situations in which teacher and pupils can
find themselves.

This variation in the management patterns of the classroom calls for considerable flexibility and ingenuity on the
part of the teacher, particularly since he is very likely to be
working in some areas unfamiliar to him or with colleagues from
other disciplines. For some experienced teachers such a change
in management style can cause difficulties and they may adjust
by modifying the particular teaching programme in such a way
that its integrative impact is lessened (Hamilton, 1975).

b) *Integration and School Management*

While integration can affect the social structure of the classroom, it can have even more serious effects on the management structure of the school. This is particularly so in secondary schools which are often organised on a subject basis.

Where there is strong boundary maintenance between subjects, power and authority reside in the head of school and in the heads of departments. Other members of staff derive their duties and responsibilities from them. Their main professional contacts tend to be of a vertical rather than a horizontal kind, and involve for the most part only other departmental colleagues. Staff develop a sense of loyalty to their subject particularly since their main avenue of promotion lies within it or through it. They therefore have a personal interest in maintaining and furthering the subject image. For a head of department such power is something of a mixed blessing, for, while he has authority in his own subject area, his authority in the school is constrained by that of his colleagues in other departments. On issues such as time-tabling and rooming he will in all probability have to compromise in the face of stronger claims from other subjects. In such a situation the head of the school exercises and maintains his power and authority by regulating the degree of disequilibrium that characterises subject differentiation in its institutionalised form. As Musgrove (1973) points out, this has a restraining influence on the power of the head. Where power is distributed among stable subject departments, there is likely to be less centralised forms of organisational control.

The introduction of integration poses a threat to subject departments and affects the formal relationships between staff. Cooperation across departments becomes necessary and this can lead to changes in the hierarchical system of order and control within the school. If subject departments are not completely disbanded at least they lose their autonomy. Musgrove claims that when departments are dissolved, only the headmaster wins. Their demise almost inevitably results in an increase in his power. The promotion prospects for staff also change. They can no longer climb the professional ladder through their subjects but must compete with colleagues from many different subjects. This not only increases the degree of competition but changes the criteria for advancement from academic to management criteria. Since many staff are neither trained nor inclined to compete on such a basis, the situation can become a source of threat, anxiety and insecurity.

To support his thesis Musgrove compares the curricular organisation and management structures of primary and secondary schools. The extent to which subjects are emphasised is a determinant of the power of the head. In primary schools where integrated approaches are more common, the head wields greater power than in secondary schools which are normally much more subject-based.

There can be little doubt that there is considerable validity in Musgrove's argument at a gross, institutional level. The adoption, to any considerable degree, of one form of curriculum organisation or another incorporates specific patterns of power and authority that affect the management and organisational structure of the school. From the point of view of the interpretation of integration presented here, however, both Musgrove's and Bernstein's theses, despite their different orientations, present some difficulties.

In the first place, they imply that subjects and integration are antithetic, whereas they are in fact complementary. The difference is that while they are viewing integration in terms of its frequent social effects, it has been discussed here from the point of view of its epistemological, psychological and educational characteristics, and in terms of its social requirements and possibilities.

Secondly, the problems of which they speak tend to occur in their most severe form in total transformations of whole school curricula. The introduction of mild forms of integration within limited areas of the curriculum, as often happens in schools, makes many such problems far less intractable.

Thirdly, they tend to view integration as a uniform phenomenon. Its many different varieties are largely subsumed under the one heading. The many different types of integration discussed in Chapter 2 vary considerably in their effects on the school as an institution.

Fourthly, they give little consideration to possible alternative patterns of school organisation capable of incorporating integrated approaches.

The most obvious recent development in this connection, particularly in middle and secondary schools, is the creation

of faculties in place of departments. These are often based on
a broad fields concept and involve the grouping of subjects,
which can contribute to a common field of study, in one administrative unit. Thus the New Zealand scheme quoted on page 36
as an example of holistic synthesis could be organised on the
basis of five faculties. The environment faculty in this instance would comprise the sciences and geography. Such a form
of organisation can allow for subject contributions but at the
same time facilitate inter-subject collaboration. It provides
a reasonable basis for the distribution of responsibility and
the allocation of time and resources (Scottish Education Department Consultative Committee on the Curriculum, 1977). In a situation in which the overcrowding of the curriculum is a threat
to some subjects, the faculty structure is seen by some as a
means of survival (Moore, 1975).

Other forms of administrative innovation which reflect an
integrative approach are the growth of certain areas of responsibility in schools which have no subject basis. These would
include posts involving specific types of integrated work such
as modern studies (Dunlop, 1977), or posts related to specific
developments in schools such as the raising of the school leaving age or the provision of remedial facilities (Haigh, 1975).
On the basis of such evidence it may be that the adoption of
integrated schemes encourages rather than eradicates the kind
of intellectual and organisational pluralism that Musgrove
(1973) cherishes.

5.3   Integration and the Administrative Structure of the School

Integration not only affects the way in which people inter-
act in the school setting; it also influences the way in which
the school is organised for educational purposes. It affects
the use of time, the use of space and the use of resources.

a)   Integration and the Use of Time

The time-table embodies in organisational form the particular curriculum structure adopted in a school. In the case of
a school which offers a subject-based curriculum, the subject
concept is encapsulated in its time-table. Subject fragmentation and a period-based time-table go hand in hand. The number
of periods allocated to a subject can also indicate something
of the status of the subject in the school.

The adoption of integrated approaches can have profound effects on the time-table and the interrelationship of the two can help to explain the various ways in which integration proposals are received in schools (Luke, 1971). If the proposals necessitate too drastic a change in the time-table, they may well be dropped. If, on the other hand, the time-table is overloaded by a proliferation of subjects, some form of integration may well be adopted to alleviate the position (Blum, 1973). Or if it is felt that the dislocated school day presents an inadequate picture of reality, a more structured and coherent form may be adopted to improve the image (Trump and Baynham, 1961). It is likely, however, that most innovations are introduced for a mixture of reasons, some philosophical, some practical.

Time-table difficulties are dependent not only upon the type and degree of integration but upon the kind of school in which it is introduced. In a primary school where the teacher largely controls her own time-table few difficulties may arise. This may even be the case in such extensive reorganisation as an integrated day, provided other variables such as accommodation, resources and provision for specialist subjects can be controlled. More limited forms of integration such as topic or project work are even more easily dealt with and can be introduced with the minimum of difficulty from a time-table point of view.

The position in subject-based middle or secondary schools is more serious. To accommodate most forms of integrated studies, particularly in parallel with subject studies, some form of blocked time-table is necessary (Nicholls, 1973). Unless staff are made available to work together in a team teaching situation, reversion to yet another form of subject teaching is likely to occur. Where complete restructuring of the curriculum is involved, a total reorganisation of the time-table on a block basis would probably be required.

   b) Integration and the Use of Space

The use of space is another important factor in integrated programmes. Just as integration can to some extent be achieved by manipulating the time-table, so it can be partly promoted by the reorganisation of space. The integrated day, for example, is simply a way of organising the curriculum on the basis of space rather than time. The subjects are still there but they are represented by positions in the classroom rather than by periods in the time-table.

Many schools are built with the various classrooms arranged in box-like fashion either in a line or round a central
hall. Such rooms were built with a particular number of children in mind and in the expectation that they would be sitting
at desks arranged in rows. Today this arrangement is frequently modified to produce clusters of tables at which children can
work in small groups, but the end result is often an overcrowded
classroom in which movement is restricted. While such an arrangement is probably better for integrated work than rows of
desks, it is by no means ideal.

The ideal will again depend on what one wishes to do, but
in the case of an integrated studies programme, in say the humanities, some form of flexible-type accommodation that can be
used or adapted for different learning purposes would be desirable. To overcome lack of suitable accommodation, Williams
(1973) for example, obtained the use of a number of humanities
rooms which were arranged round a central reference area.
Other reports speak of similar arrangements. A Team of Staff
from Llanederyn High School, Cardiff, Wales (1972) developed an
integrated studies area, which had movable walls and was composed of a lecture theatre surrounded by work areas with craft
facilities. In such a situation the centrality of a resource
area is important.

At a more humble level it would seem sensible to aim for
a flexible classroom in which the furniture can be arranged
with the minimum of effort, preferably by the children themselves, so that a variety of appropriate teaching-learning situations can be readily created. Children should have ample
room in which to work so that they do not disturb each other
unduly, and the teacher should have sufficient accommodation
for housing resources and displaying work.

In most schools such ideal conditions are seldom available and some kind of compromise is almost always necessary if
integrated work is to be done at all. This requires the imag-
inative creation of alternatives and sometimes these can have
advantages over initially more appealing and sophisticated
practices. In countries where the weather and other conditions
are favourable, for example, the community should become the
learning space for the school instead of the school remaining
the learning space for the community.

c) Integration and the Use of Resources

From the point of view of integration the term 'resources' refers to a very wide range of provision. It includes the staff of the school, library and audiovisual-aid facilities and equipment, work materials, school accommodation and furniture, and provision for learning in the environment and community. It is this extensive use of every available resource for learning that in many ways characterises integrated teaching. Implicit in the idea of such teaching is the integration of every conceivable form of educational provision. In the context of integrated teaching such provision comprises human, material and community resources.

The centrality of human resources arises from the cooperative nature of integrated work and its reliance on the disciplines of knowledge. Andain and Johnson (1973) maintain that an integrated course can be fitted into a conventional timetable provided the staff are committed and enthusiastic. But if there is no cooperation, there can be no integration. The primary requirement, therefore, is to win the confidence and obtain the assistance of all concerned. Only on such a basis can the contributions from the various disciplines be assured, for these are mediated through people and largely determine in many instances the educational validity of the whole enterprise.

The practical nature of integrated work depends on the availability of material resources. Without them learning becomes a theoretical exercise and reversion to the book learning of traditional subject teaching becomes inevitable. Materials help to pull teaching and learning as close to reality as possible, and often the more natural the materials the closer the link becomes. Even so, a great many teaching materials convey experience second hand and these constitute a vast reserve of educational potential. A number of writers recommend the bringing together of books, pamphlets, leaflets, pictures, posters, photographs, tapes, films, slides and other equipment in a centrally located integrated studies resource area (Gilliatt, 1974; Hinds, 1974).

Material resources represent the process of bringing the real world into the school; the use of community resources represents the process of bringing the school out into the real world. This latter movement is particularly important in integrated work because of the practical and often social nature of many of the issues with which it deals. The environment and

community in which the school is situated can provide a fund of
educational experience which under the old, traditional system
tended to remain unused. The evidence suggests that work of an
integrated or interdisciplinary kind is helping to strengthen
the educational link between school and the world outside (e.g.
Lamb, et al, 1973).

5.4   Knowledge and System

This chapter has shown that the way in which knowledge is
organised for curriculum purposes and the administrative structure of the system that provides the curriculum are inexorably
interwined. It has also suggested that the micro-system of the
school is but part of the macro-system of society and that the
child at his desk in the schoolroom is, as it were, at the ful-
crum of these various interacting forces that characterise the
social organisation of knowledge. The pressure to retain the
subject system and the pressure to dismantle it in favour of
some form of integrated structure meet in the curriculum that
schools provide for children. The message of this chapter
would seem to be that there is no easy way of resolving the difficulties which such a power struggle creates, a point that
will be elaborated in the next chapter. In concluding this
one, however, it must be pointed out that many of the difficulties arise from the failure of each of the opposing parties to
recognise the validity of the other's case. Until such time as
integrated and subject teaching are seen to serve complementary
purposes in the life of the individual, administrative matters
will continue to subvert the educational functions that could
otherwise be served.

CHAPTER 6

PROBLEMS AND PROSPECTS

6.1 Vision and Reality

Although the discussion has made much distinction between integrated and subject approaches, it was stressed in Chapter 2 that these are not antithetical but complementary, the one being an extension of the principles, procedures and practices of the other. In considering the concept of integration and the various educational issues that it raises, the arguments have been strongly in its favour and may be considered to have presented a one-sided point of view. This is perhaps inevitable in such a discussion but it should not obscure either the strengths of subjects or the weaknesses of integration. Much of the dialogue and many of the opinions held in this field are highly charged emotionally and indicative of a fervour and fanaticism that leave little room for professional judgement of a rational kind (Esland, 1971). There can be little doubt that such extremism in whatever form, does not in the end benefit children. In the teaching-learning situation vision and reality should always coalesce and this cannot happen when judgement is suspended by emotion. In the pages which follow an attempt will be made to provide a more critical assessment of curriculum integration by presenting some of the principal problems which it poses, and appraising its prospects in the educational enterprise. This will be done by looking at the implications of integration for knowledge, for society and for people.

6.2 Integration and Knowledge

Some of the main difficulties created by curriculum integration stem from the questions that it raises concerning traditional views of knowledge. Essentially these questions involve the relationship between the origins of knowledge in ex-

perience and the product of knowing in culture. Knowledge is
created through progressive fragmentation and dissociation from
its origins in experience, and the more there is to know the
more difficult it becomes to understand knowledge through re-
discovery of its experiential roots. Integration is fundamentally concerned with the process of rediscovering the foundations of knowledge in experience, and making the edifice of
knowledge meaningful for life. Four problems created by this
process will be discussed. The first concerns integration and
the structure of knowledge.

a) Integration and the Structure of Knowledge

The development of knowledge in recent years has been
achieved by progressive specialisation and this has meant that
the structure of knowledge has become increasingly differentiated and fragmented. Though integration does not involve a
reversal of this process, it represents an attempt to counteract its dissociative effects. The more knowledge is advanced,
the less coherent it becomes, and this means that, though particular areas of knowledge are better understood, knowledge as
a whole becomes less meaningful. While this process improves
our knowledge, it makes the business of education, which is
basically concerned with helping the child to make sense of his
world, all the more difficult.

It is perhaps not coincidental, therefore, that the increase in the quantity of knowledge has been accompanied by
considerable debate on the question of structure as an aspect
of both learning and teaching. Educationists are concerned to
identify and trace the complex interrelationships and basic patterns that underlie the diversity of knowledge and the process
of knowing in today's world. One attempt to do this (Hirst,
1974) will be examined to illustrate the kind of problems that
integration poses for the structure of knowledge. It will be
recalled (see p. 31) that Hirst detects in knowledge a limited
number of discrete, logical patterns which he calls forms of
knowledge. Each form is distinguished by its conceptual structure and its ways of knowing. In all, there are probably five
to seven forms comprising mathematics, physical science, ethics,
religion, aesthetics, and probably history and the human sciences. In addition to the forms there are an unlimited number
of fields of knowledge which are defined not by their logical
coherence but by the nature of their subject matter. These include subjects such as geography, home economics, medicine and
even project or topic work. To understand such areas, use is

made of the forms of knowledge and it is the forms rather than
the fields that determine the nature of what it means to be educated.

In Hirst's model, integration is a characteristic of the
fields rather than the forms, though he seems to imply that the
fields should be based on the forms and contribute to an understanding of their interrelationship (Hirst and Peters, 1970).
This leaves unsolved the problem of integrating the forms or
disciplines of knowledge and raises a number of questions about
the structure of knowledge implied in Hirst's model. Is it the
case that the essential structure of experience is only truly
reflected in the logical patterns of thought? Are these logical patterns as distinct as Hirst implies, or are there other
ways of organising the structure of knowledge on an experiential
basis that would make a greater degree of curriculum integration possible? Considering Hirst's own doubts about the number
of forms and the very large variety of alternative ways of structuring knowledge proposed by other writers (e.g. Macmurray, 1936;
Snow, 1959; Rogers, 1964; Phenix, 1964; Broudy, Smith and
Burnett, 1964; Tykociner, 1964), it would seem unwise on the
basis of any one of them to place restrictions on either subject teaching or the possibilities of integration. Until a
more generally acceptable conceptual structure for knowledge is
available, which allows for the distinctiveness and complex interrelationship of its principal elements, such structural problems in curriculum integration will remain unsolved.

b) *The Articulation of Subject and Integrated Teaching*

One of the practical problems arising from the structural
issue, is that of articulating subject and integrated teaching.
This implies that some element of both is necessary in every
curriculum, a view that has quite wide support (e.g. Hirst and
Peters, 1970). Subject and integrated teaching should be
mutually reinforcing. The problem here, however, is not
just how the curriculum can incorporate these two very different approaches to knowledge, but how their respective contributions can be best coordinated in the interests of the educational
development of children. To deal with this problem it is necessary to identify those factors that shape the pattern of subject and integrated teaching in the curriculum.

In the first place, age and its associated levels of learning would seem to be significant factors in determining both the
extent and type of integration appropriate for different groups

of children. In the early years a functional approach on quite
an extensive scale would seem to be conducive to learning.
Hence the relatively unstructured nature of the nursery classroom and the popularity of the integrated day in infant schools.
In the junior years integration, perhaps in the form of topic
or project work, would seem to provide the kind of practical
learning experiences that one would associate with the stage
of concrete operational thinking. At the secondary level the
growth of formal thought apparently necessitates increasing
subject differentiation, and this in turn calls for some form
of structural integration of an interdisciplinary kind. Thus
many integrated courses in the humanities, science and social
studies for example respect the individuality of subjects but
attempt to present them in a more coordinated and coherent form.
At the more advanced levels of disciplinary thought which are
normally reached in late adolescence or early manhood, when in
the lives of individuals practical application as well as a
coherent outlook assume greater significance, the relevance of
integration again increases. Thus many university undergradu-
ates and those who start work have a vocational focus which
helps to give meaning to their various learning activities. And
adolescence would seem to be a time when many young people attempt to find meaning in their lives by seeking a synoptic view
of the universe such as is found in religion. The years of
childhood and youth would, therefore, seem to be characterised
by cycles of development in which differentiation and integration of learning experiences are variously emphasised.

Another factor would appear to be the nature of subjects
and the ways in which they are taught. In geography, for example, which draws its data from the sciences and the humanities,
integrative possibilities would seem to fit more readily into
the teaching of the subject, than in the case of, say, mathematics. Whitfield (1971) argues that real integration is possible at present only within the sciences and art and crafts,
the area of the humanities being problematic. There is, ad-
ditionally, the view that some subjects have much greater integrative capacity than others, though such a view seems to be
partly determined by commitment to the subject. Heater (1972),
for example, argues for history as a synoptic subject, whereas
Dineen (1969) argues for linguistics, Lancashire (1973) for
theology, and Markham (1970) for philosophy.

Again, integration would seem to depend to some extent on
the balance of different subjects or disciplines within the curriculum. A curriculum that had a bias towards one area of knowl-

edge rather than another might be integrated in the sense of presenting a coherent point of view, but it would probably be less integrative than a more rounded curriculum which provided appropriately for the development of the many different facets of the personality. On the other hand, a comprehensive, subject-based curriculum which included within it an integrated programme, would simply reduce integration to another subject.

Finally, the effects of integration on different subjects vary and this also exacerbates the articulation problem. For example, Bull (1968) points out that geography as a science-humanities subject suffers from being incorporated in a humanities programme because of its high scientific content. In a science programme it could well suffer a similar fate, and the difficulty here would be to find an integrated structure in which an already integrated subject could make an appropriate contribution.

c) *Breadth and Depth of Knowledge*

Integration tends to promote breadth of knowledge, although, by probing the deep structures of the disciplines, it should also increase depth of understanding. Specialisation, on the other hand produces a depth of knowledge and understanding in a narrow area, but at higher levels links with other subjects also become possible. In practice, however, such merging of the functions of specialist and integrated teaching often does not occur. Integrated teaching, as Knox (1961) observes, tends to produce superficial coverage over a broad area with a consequent loss of consolidation within the disciplines. This is a concern which is expressed frequently in the literature (Pilley, 1959; Holt, 1964; Taylor, 1971; Choat, 1974).

The association of integration with breadth of knowledge makes it a feature of the debate on general and specialist education. It figures prominently, in the discussion of a core curriculum as providing a minimum general education (e.g. Unesco, 1968; Unesco, 1975a; Lawton, 1969). It is also one of the principal characteristics of the American concept of a core curriculum as a programme of studies which demonstrates the applicability of school subjects to personal issues and social problems (Billett, 1970).

The broadening of the curriculum, however, through integration exacerbates the existing problem of enabling teachers, who are either general practitioners or specialist trained, to

cope with areas of knowledge in integrated teaching with which
they themselves are perhaps not too familiar (Salt, 1969).

d) *Progressive Ordering of Content*

While subjects are well-structured and suited to progres-
sion, many integrated activities are haphazard and disordered.
This makes it very difficult for the teacher in the integrated
context to ensure that his pupils are in fact making adequate
progress in each of the different areas of educational development. Logical order is a clearer guide than psychological order and good teaching depends on an appropriate blend of the
two. Careful and systematic recording of children's progress
can do much to mitigate this difficulty.

An associated danger is that of repetition or duplication
of work covered, particularly in circumstances where there is
little vertical integration either between classes in the same
school or between schools for different age levels. Bull (1968)
draws attention to this difficulty in environmental studies. A
child moving from a primary to a secondary school in the same
locality can find himself involved in activities in an environmental studies course which are little better than a repeat performance of what he did in primary school. This kind of difficulty can only be solved by effective communication and close
liaison not only within schools but between schools.

6.3   Integration and Society

Any form of educational activity has social implications,
integration no less than any other. Three types of social issue related to curriculum integration have been selected for
comment. They are integration and national educational policy,
integration and the examination system, and integration and
political action.

a) *Integration and National Educational Policy*

Because there is no one way of integrating the curriculum,
responsibility for integration rests very heavily on the teacher. He must decide what particular form is most appropriate in
the circumstances, taking into consideration such factors as
the needs of individual pupils, the facilities in the school
and the nature of the local environment. Integration lacks the
public consensus inherent in subjects and the ways in which it

is implemented often tend to be idiosyncratic (Fisher, 1972).

For this reason it is difficult to lay down a structure for integration on a large scale. Much depends on the freedom of the teacher to determine an appropriate curriculum for his own pupils. Where this freedom is controlled in whatever way by national policy or traditional procedures, the constraints on the teacher can militate against the adoption of integrative approaches.

The amount of freedom that the teacher can exercise in controlling the curriculum varies from country to country. In the United Kingdom, for example, the teacher has very considerable freedom to organise the work of his class as he pleases, and consequently he can decide how much integration, if any, is appropriate for his pupils. On the continent of Europe there is, in national terms, much less freedom of action because European nations on the whole tend to exercise greater centralised control over what is taught in schools. If the national curriculum does not include integrated activities, then they are not likely to be adopted in individual instances.

The British system, however, presents a dilemma for the curriculum planner. If teachers can, comparatively speaking, do as they please, they are just as likely to decide against curriculum integration as for it. Unless there is some professional consensus on the place of integration in education, provision for it is likely to remain problematic.

b) *Integration and the Examination System*

Examination systems for the most part presuppose a subject approach to teaching. Quite apart from epistemological considerations, this makes for ease of administration and fits the matriculation system for entry to university. The tendency, at least in secondary schools, has been to adopt a form of curriculum organisation which meets the requirements of higher education.

Evidence from a number of countries suggests that the subject orientation of the examination system discourages the adoption of integrated approaches in school. Krasilchik (1975), for example, reports that teachers in Brazil were sometimes unwilling to embark on integrated science projects because the proposed courses did not prepare pupils for entrance to university. Similar reports emanate from Kenya, the United Kingdom and Malaysia (Hopkin, 1971; Gregson and Quinn, 1972; Kooi, 1975). The removal of such an academic and subject emphasis on the school curriculum at the secondary level would seem to depend on some modification in university entrance procedures (C.E.R.I., 1972).

During the life of the individual, the years in which he prepares for entrance to university are the ones in which there is greatest resistance to integration. Preparation for the professions, for example medicine, law, engineering, agriculture, apparently requires a subject approach to learning. The question that arises from this is whether the influence brought to bear on the educational system as a whole by such a minority is justified.

   c) *Integration and Political Action*

   The previous two sections dealt with the social influences on integration at the national level. In this section consideration is given to the political activity that integration tends to engender within institutions.

   In the first place the introduction of integrated courses is often seen as a threat by those in subject departments. This is understandable, because such courses can in some instances herald the demise of departments. Thus Doyal's (1974) finding at the university level that professional subject interests often operate in such a way as to constrict the development of integrated work, reflects what often happens in schools. The factors which decide whether or not staff will cooperate are not always educational. Jenkins and Shipman (1976) speak of teachers who will join an integrated studies programme only if promotion is available through it.

   A more serious danger occurs when individuals within an institution seize upon integration as a useful political instrument for increasing their power, improving their status, or consolidating their position. There are those who will use integration as a means of self-advancement, as Sellick (1975) reports. This can have considerable repercussions for the individuals in the institution if the technique is used, say to dismantle a departmental structure in order to achieve a different pattern of power and authority. There is little doubt that integration can be used as an impressive excuse for such covertly political manipulation of educational institutions. Whether such behaviour has any professional or educational validity is a moot point.

6.4   Integration and People

It should be clear by now that integration is for people; it is person-centred. If it does not function as a means of improving the quality of the educational experiences offered in our schools, it may remain as an interesting idea, but be of little practical and personal consequence to our pupils. Only as a means to more effective learning can it be justified as an approach to better teaching. It has validity only if it serves an educational purpose by helping pupils and improving teachers.

a) *Curriculum Integration and Educational Purpose*

Curriculum integration is introduced into schools for all sorts of reasons and such variety of justification is under-standable in view of the wide range of possibilities open to the teacher. There are occasions, however, when the real rea-son for its introduction cannot be justified in educational terms and in such circumstances teachers often use it without really knowing what they are doing (Esland, 1971). It is as a consequence of such action that integration is accused of dil-ettantism (Wise, 1966), gimmickry and superficiality (Connelly, 1972) and of being generally ineffectual (Taylor, 1971).

There are other occasions when integration is used appar-ently for valid educational reasons, but in such a way that ex-cludes the possibility of other necessary educational approaches being used. This happens, for example, when it is unsupported by and lends little support to the disciplines, as we discussed in connection with breadth and depth of knowledge.

In both these cases integration fails to fulfil purposes appropriate to the educational development of persons and its use in these circumstances is unjustified. It is important that the teacher should be capable of deciding the degree and type of integration that will be of greatest educational bene-fit to his pupils on any particular occasion. Professional justification lies in the primacy of the pupil as a person, not in the predilections of teachers or the characteristics of spe-cial systems.

b) Curriculum Integration and the Pupil

Integration, then, is a pupil-centred activity. Its basic
purpose is not to present to the world an impressively coherent
curriculum but to help pupils to develop the ability to integrate knowledge for themselves and enable them through such a
process, to find meaning in what they learn. Three aspects of
integrated teaching are cause for concern from the point of
view of its personal orientation.

Firstly, one of the principal tenets of integrative education is that the child should learn for himself. Self-directed
learning is one of the concomitants of integrative teaching.
The development of the capacity to learn stems from the intention to teach as much as from the motivation to learn. This is
particularly so in the case of integrated teaching with its
emphasis on choice and its penetration to the deep structures
of knowledge.

Secondly, self-directed learning can place a very large
measure of responsibility on the child for his own learning.
All children do not possess in equal measure either the capacity or the motivation to fulfil this responsibility. Some may
find it too heavy a burden and in such cases the teacher must
act vicariously to ensure the growth of confidence and indepen-
dence.

Thirdly, it is frequently stated that while integrated
work is suitable for the average or below average child, subject studies are more appropriate for able children (e.g. Hirst,
1969; Lamb et al., 1973; Jones, 1975). This viewpoint has many
doubtful implications. It implies that integrated work is easy
and not sufficiently taxing for the bright child, a point of
view challenged by Nicholls (1973). It implies that there are
two kinds of knowledge, two ways of knowing, one for the bright
and one for the dull. Not only does this dichotomise subject
and integrated teaching, but it also divides education into two
systems, as Shipman (1971) observes.

c) Curriculum Integration and the Teacher

Some teachers do not like integration and see it as a
threat to their subject or to the ways in which they have traditionally conducted their classes. Others do not like subjects
and view integration as a sort of educational panacea. The
first group are most strongly concentrated in the secondary

school, the second in the primary school. Integration and subjects are thus to some extent institutionalised in primary and
secondary education. In recent years, however, integration has
been increasingly introduced into secondary schools (Pring,
1971) and for many teachers may be a source of anxiety and insecurity.

Such uncertainty stems not just from fear of loss of authority and prestige but from the difficulty that practically
all teachers encounter in contributing to interdisciplinary
courses involving relatively unfamiliar areas of knowledge.
This difficulty increases as one progresses from the compara-
tive simplicity of an infant school programme to the undoubted
complexity of the secondary school curriculum. The global perspective is comparatively easy at a simple level, and probably
also at a very advanced level, but, at the intermediate level
of academic work in school, both the comprehensiveness of the
general practitioner and the profundity of the specialist are
something of a disadvantage.

This has implications for both in-service and pre-service
teacher education. The threat of innovation is considerably
reduced by sympathetic understanding and the provision of appropriate informational and educational services. Teachers
should not be expected to participate in teaching schemes that
are unfamiliar to them without the support of some kind of in-
service training. This can be provided by colleagues in the
school, by teachers' centres or by local colleges.

Training in integrated work should also play a significant
part in pre-service teacher education. As might be expected it
has for many years been a feature of the training of infant and
primary school teachers, though its position in courses is very
much determined by the professional attitudes predominant in individual institutions. The problem is probably most severe at
the graduate level and consideration is being given to the possibility of introducing degrees in interdisciplinary studies
(Doyal, 1974; Brunsdon, 1976). Perhaps this will assist in developing in subject departments of universities an awareness of
their role in teacher education, though its immediate implications for integrated work in schools remains to be seen.

6.5   Integration, Institutionalisation and Individualisation

It could be said that subjects represent knowledge in its

institutionalised form whereas integration is characterised by
many features of knowledge in its personalised form. The one
reflects the public image of knowledge, the other the private
image. The tendency in the one is to depersonalise knowledge,
in the other to repersonalise it. The result is what has already been described as the uncommonsense knowledge of the
school and the commonsense knowledge of the everyday world.
Such a dichotomy is, of course, a mental reconstruction of reality and, as such, suffers from the weaknesses of generalisation, but it nevertheless points to the source of the kind of
problems that have been discussed in this chapter. These stem
from the tension between the depersonalisation of knowledge in
culture and the repersonalisation of knowledge in education.
Subject teaching tends to have an affinity with the one process,
and integrated teaching with the other.

As things stand at the moment there are pros and cons in
both subject and integrated teaching and it is the teacher's
task to achieve some kind of rapprochement within the curriculum and within the institution of the school that best serves
the educational interests of individual children. Clearly this
is not an easy task.

CHAPTER 7

TOWARDS LIFELONG
INTEGRATION

This concluding chapter reviews what was said at the outset about lifelong education and curriculum integration and
leads to an appraisal of the place of subjects and integration
in lifelong education. The chapter also views curriculum integration from the larger perspective of integration in life,
thus giving it a personal and community focus and not just an
educational one. Such a lifelong perspective gives added meaning and deeper significance to an otherwise confined pedagogical procedure.

7.1 Integration, Subjects and Life

It was suggested in Chapter 1 that lifelong education and
curriculum integration share a number of common educational ideals, and it could be assumed from this that integrated teaching
is particularly relevant to lifelong education. In this connection three questions need to be answered. Firstly, are the
statements on the similarity of the goals of curriculum integration and lifelong education posited in Chapter 1 justified?
Secondly, how useful is curriculum integration as a practical
outlet for lifelong education? Thirdly, what is the role of
subjects in lifelong education? An attempt will be made to answer each of these in turn.

a) The Similarity between the Goals of Lifelong
Education and Curriculum Integration

The hypothesis on which this study was based was, that
from an ideological point of view, curriculum integration and
lifelong education have much in common. Eight areas of general
educational interest but of particular significance for both
curriculum integration and lifelong education were identified.

94

These were concerned with the links between change and educational development, the interrelationship of school and society and the need for an open approach to education, a utilitarian approach to knowledge, an operational purpose in learning, a cooperative interpretation of teaching, emphasis on the individual in education and the continuous enhancement of educability. As a consequence it was hypothesised that curriculum integration and lifelong education might well be of benefit to each other. Lifelong education with its theoretical orientation might gain a practical outlet, and curriculum integration with its practical bias might profit from greater theoretical justification. Such was the hope. To what extent was it justified?

Though reiteration of the details of the arguments supporting such an assumption would at this stage be tedious, it might be helpful to bring together under each heading some of the principal examples of the evidence presented.

1) *Education for Change*

Integration has been portrayed as a reflection in school of the changes currently taking place in society (pp. 22 and 71 ff.), as a means of dealing with changes in knowledge (pp. 22, 44 ff., 78 and 82 ff.) and a way of preparing children to cope with contemporary social problems (pp. 40 ff. and 54 ff.).

2) *School and Society*

The interrelationship of school and society is a basic principle underlying a great deal of integrated work. It is a characteristic of many functional types (pp. 39 ff.), forms the basis for the social functions (pp. 54 ff.) and is implied in the principles of integrative learning (pp. 63 ff.).

3) *Open Education*

Many of the strengths and weaknesses of integration stem from its open approach to education and the curriculum (pp. 39 and 87). Whereas subjects are considered to be closed systems of thought (pp. 72 ff.), functional types of integration in particular are characterised by openness (pp. 37 ff.). This is also a feature of the principles of integrative learning (pp. 61 ff.) and of the practice of creative teaching (pp. 65 ff.).

4) *Knowledge that is Useful*

The need for knowledge to be useful is a principle that has been advocated throughout the study. Functional types of integration view knowledge as a resource for living rather than as content to be learned (pp. 36 ff.). They emphasise the need for knowledge to be socially relevant (pp. 45, 54 and 55) and applicable to life (pp. 49 and 50, 63 and 64, and 72).

5) *Operational Learning*

The concept of operational learning is implicit in many types of integration (pp. 30-37), in the psychological functions (pp. 52 ff.), in the principles of integrative learning (pp. 61 ff.), and in the notion of facilitative teaching (pp. 66 ff.).

6) *Consensus for Action*

Without consensus for action no form of integration would be possible. It is therefore a characteristic feature of the following integrative activities: interrelating different areas of knowledge (pp. 46 ff.), teaching and learning through sharing (99. 53 ff.), planning an integrated curriculum (pp. 58 ff.), and teaching cooperatively (pp. 66 and 91 ff.).

7) *The Primacy of the Person*

Evidence that integrated teaching is concerned with the all-round development of the personality and the individualisation of learning is given in the discussion of functional types (pp. 37 ff.), purpose in knowledge (pp. 47-48), psychological functions (pp. 49 ff.), principles of integrative learning (pp. 61 ff.), criterion-referenced assessment (pp. 67-68) and integration and people (pp. 90 ff.).

8) *Enhancement of Educability*

Evidence that this is of particular concern to curriculum integration was provided by the analysis of intrinsic forms of motivation (p. 49) and in the importance attached to personal growth, self-actualisation and self-directed learning (pp. 50 ff.), to creative and productive thinking (p. 62) and to facilitative teaching (p. 66).

Such evidence would seem to confirm the preliminary statements made in Chapter 1 that, in general terms, curriculum inte-

gration and lifelong education are compatible. In theory, at
least, curriculum integration is capable of providing learning
experiences conducive to lifelong education. However, in view
of the typology of curriculum integration developed in Chapter
2, and the complementarity established between curriculum integration and subject teaching, it cannot be maintained that all
forms of curriculum integration make an equally significant contribution to lifelong education, or that subject teaching is
thereby precluded from making any.

b) Curriculum Integration as a Practical Outlet for the Principles of Lifelong Education

While curriculum integration obviously has the potential
to promote lifelong education, the extent to which it can do
this in the practical context of the school is limited by a
number of factors. These factors include the type of integration employed, its relationship to subject teaching in the
school, the attitudes and capabilities of the teachers, the
power of the headmaster, the administrative structure of the
school, the facilities available, and so on. Though many of
these factors also affect subject teaching, the particular nature of integrated teaching is such that it often intensifies
rather than diminishes the difficulties involved. Even given
favourable conditions, integrated teaching is not easy and it
should never be regarded as an educational panacea. Unless it
is implemented in the right place at the right time and for the
right reasons, it is very likely to be educationally disadvan-
tageous. In whatever form, it requires for its successful implementation a high level of teaching skill, just as good subject teaching does. Because it represents a continuation of,
rather than a departure from the structuring of knowledge characteristic of subject teaching, it involves a degree of planning
and organisation that equals, if not exceeds, that necessary
for subject teaching.

It has to be concluded, therefore, that though curriculum
integration has a very positive contribution to make to lifelong education, the quality of that contribution is dependent
on the extent to which curriculum integration can be success-
fully implemented.

c) Lifelong Education and Subject Teaching

An important question that remains to be answered involves
the role of subjects in lifelong education. If integrated teach-

ing is relevant to lifelong education, have subjects no part to play in it? From the point of view of this study the answer to this question is quite clear: subject teaching is just as essential as integrated teaching. Several reasons can be given to support this contention.

There is first of all the logical reason. Subjects are the raison d'être of curriculum integration. Integration would not be possible if there were nothing to integrate or if what was to be integrated was incapable of integration. Knowledge without subjects, that is in its unstructured state, would not be amenable to any form of integration other than that which produced subjects in the first place. In fact many forms of integration are little more than the creation of new subject patterns. A social studies programme, for example, which combines history and geography, while it may have considerable educational advantages from the point of view of curriculum integration, is often just a new subject replacing history and geography in the curriculum. It makes little sense, logically, therefore, to think that integration is, or can be, independent of subject teaching.

This leads to the second reason, which arises from the epistemological standpoint adopted in this study. It will be recalled that curriculum integration and subject teaching were presented at the outset as complementary rather than contradictory notions. Subjects in themselves are integrated structures and integrated teaching is therefore an extension of the integrative process inherent in subject teaching. A teacher, who is competent in a variety of subjects, can provide an integrated curriculum through subject teaching by consistently tracing the integrative threads that link the subjects while teaching them. Many primary shool teachers, and some secondary ones also, teach in this way. The difficulty arises when teachers do not have sufficient knowledge to do this or when the organisation of education is such that it prevents them from doing it. It is in such circumstances that subject teaching becomes subject to formality and fails to meet the kind of educational criteria characterising curriculum integration and lifelong education.

The third reason why subject teaching is just as important for lifelong education as integrated teaching is that the difficulties in subject teaching, which integration attempts to solve, arise not so much from the subjects as such, as from some of the ways in which they are frequently taught. It can therefore be called the methodological reason. Taught in an appro-

priate manner, subjects can fulfil the most stringent educational requirements. It would seem senseless, therefore, to dispense with subjects just because they are taught badly. To do
this would be to deny children a most important part of their
educational heritage. Thus, contrary to much popular belief,
most forms of integration preserve rather than destroy the subject basis of knowledge by attempting to improve methodology
rather than eradicating subject content. The integrated day,
for example, as described on page 39, maintains the subject
image but presents it in terms of space rather than time. And
James' (1968) proposals for interdisciplinary enquiry (page 40)
are based on the retention of a strong subject element within
the curriculum.

The fourth reason for maintaining the importance of subjects in lifelong education follows from what was said previously about cognitive styles (Chapter 3). It forms what may be
called the argument from cognition. It will be recalled that
there is some evidence to suggest that people vary in the ways
in which they assimilate and accommodate information. Some
learn best by receiving and storing detailed information in
their minds, while others perfer to have information presented
in more general terms or in a more structured way. As Cropley
(1976) suggests, this means that there should be a place in
every curriculum for a variety of patterns of knowledge so that
every opportunity is provided for maximum cognitive development.
For this to happen both subject and integrated approaches are
necessary.

The fifth and final reason for endorsing the importance
of subject teaching lies in the nature of subjects as represen-
tative of experience. It may be called the experiential reason.
It is mistaken to think that because subjects present a fragmented view of knowledge, they are unrelated to the principal
dimensions of experience represented by the disciplines of knowledge. Subjects are derived from the disciplines and the disciplines originate in experience. To dispense with subjects would
be to deprive children of cognitive access to these experiential
origins of knowledge, and to keep from them the meaning for life
that they hold, particularly when viewed through the synoptic
perspective of an integrated curriculum.

For such reasons, therefore, subject teaching and integrated teaching complement each other. Their function is to be
mutually reinforcing, not mutually self-destructive. Subject
teaching should promote integrative learning; integrated teach-

ing should develop the understanding of subjects; and both should help to develop the potential and motivation for lifelong learning.

7.2   From Curriculum to Community

The principal focus in this study has been upon the significance of integration for the curriculum of schools. It has involved the examination of an aspect of the educational experience of children during the school years and integration has been presented very largely within that context. This might imply that the purpose of integration is defined by the limits of learning and teaching appropriate to school curricula. Such limits would be rather restrictive for a study with a lifelong perspective. In closing, therefore, it is necessary to look again briefly at the purposes of integration so that they can be seen in terms not just of the school curriculum but of life itself.

In this perspective the ultimate purpose of integration relates not to the work of schools but to the lives of individuals. If its influence was contained within the walls of schools it would be of little moment. Unless it can be shown to extend from the curriculum to the community, it may have significance for teaching but be devoid of meaning for life. That integration has such a transcendent purpose is clear from the four phases that can be identified in the achievement of integration, the last of which provides the main justification for the other three.

Phase one is the teaching phase and involves the continuation of the structuring of knowledge beyond subjects and disciplines. Here responsibility for integration rests largely with the teacher. It is his task to ensure that the picture of the world that he presents to children has some coherence and that it is meaningful for life. Much of what has been said in the previous pages has been concerned with this problem.

Phase two is the learning phase and involves the development of integrative capacity in children. Here the child is directly involved in the cognitive structuring of his experience and it is the teacher's job to assist him in this process. Since each child will do this in his own way, the teacher must adopt an individualised approach to teaching and learning so that the child can learn how to differentiate and how to integrate his experience for himself.

The importance of individuality is at a premium in phase three. This is the personality phase and involves the coherence and integrity of the personality. To become a whole person the child must see his life in a world setting. He must be able to reconcile his own existence with that of the universe. Integrated teaching can offer him considerable assistance in developing such a world view.

The culmination of this whole process of integration is achieved in phase four. This is the community phase and involves the harmonising of human relationships and the creation of community. It is in counteracting the divisiveness of knowledge in community terms that curriculum integration finds its ultimate justification. In this respect it corroborates Macmurray's (1957) dictum that all meaningful knowledge is for the sake of action and all meaningful action is for the sake of friendship. By promoting friendship curriculum integration achieves its lifelong goal.

Viewed from a lifelong perspective curriculum integration makes an important contribution to educational progress, personality development and the fostering of community. In these roles it serves not just to improve teaching but to enhance living. Far from being simply a teaching technique, it is an essential feature of any curriculum that prepares children for life.

REFERENCES

Acland, R. *A Move to the Integrated Curriculum*. Exeter, Great Britain: University of Exeter, Institute of Education, 1967. (Themes in Education No.7).

Andain, I. and Johnson, S. "History and geography - an experiment in integration". *Teaching History*, 3 (1973), pp. 121-125.

Apple, M.W. "Community, knowledge and the structure of disciplines". *The Educational Forum*, 37 (1972), pp. 75-82.

Auld R. *William Tyndale Junior and Infants Schools Public Enquiry*. London: Inner London Education Authority, 1976.

Ausubel, D.P. "A cognitive-structure theory of school learning". In Siegel, L. (ed.). *Instruction: Some Contemporary Viewpoints*. San Francisco: Chandler, 1967.

Bellack, A.A. and Kliebard, H.M. "Curriculum for integration of disciplines". In Deighton, L.C. (ed.). *The Encyclopedia of Education*. New York: Macmillan, 1971.

Benjamin, H. *The Cultivation of Idiosyncrasy*. Cambridge, Mass.: Harvard University Press, 1949.

Bennett, N. *Teaching Styles and Pupil Progress*. London: Open Books, 1976.

Bernstein, B. "Open schools, open society". *New Society*, (14th September, 1967).

Bernstein, B. "On the classification and framing of educational knowledge". In Young, M.F.D. *Knowledge and Control*. London: Collier-Macmillan, 1971.

Biggs, J.B. "Content to process". *Australian Journal of Education*, 17 (1973), pp. 225-238.

Billett, R.O. *Improving the Secondary School Curriculum*. A Guide to Effective Curriculum Planning. New York: Atherton Press, 1970.

Bloom, B.S. "Ideas, problems and methods of inquiry". In Henry, N.B. (ed.). *The Integration of Educational Experiences*. The Fifty-Seventh Yearbook of the National Society for the Study of Education, Part III. Chicago, Illinois: University of Chicago Press, 1958.

Bloom, B.S.; Engelhardt, M.D.; Furst, E.; Hill, W.H. and Kratwohl, D.R. *Taxonomy of Educational Objectives: Handbook I: Cognitive Domain*. New York: Longmans Green, 1956.

Blum, A. "Towards a rationale for integrated science teaching". In Richmond, P.E. (ed.). *New Trends in Integrated Science Teaching*. Vol.II. Paris: Unesco, 1973.

Blyth, A.; Cooper, K.; Derricott, R.; Elliott, G.; Sumner, H. and Walpington, A. *Place, Time and Society, 8-13: Curriculum Planning in History, Geography and Social Science*. Bristol: Collins E.S.L. for the Schools Council, 1975.

Bolam, D.W. "Integrating the curriculum - a case study in the humanities". *Paedagogica Europaea*, VI (1970-71), pp. 157-171.

Bolam, D.W. "The Keele integrated studies project: four footnotes". *General Education*, 18 (1972), pp. 14-18.

Broudy, H.; Smith, B.O. and Burnett, W. *Democracy and Excellence in American Education*. Chicago: Rand McNally, 1964.

Brown, M. and Precious, N. *The Integrated Day in the Primary School*. London: Ward Lock, 1968.

Bruner, J.S. *The Process of Education*. Chicago, Illinois: Harvard University Press, 1960.

Bruner, J.S. *Toward a Theory of Instruction*. Chicago, Illinois: Harvard University Press, 1967.

Brunsdon, P. "Towards a bachelor of interdisciplinary studies degree". *Education and Training*, 18 (1976), pp. 291-292.

Bull, G.B.G. "Interdisciplinary enquiry: a geography teacher's assessment". *Geography*, 53 (1968), pp. 381-386.

C.E.R.I. (Centre for Educational Research and Innovation). *The Nature of the Curriculum for the Eighties and Onwards*. Report of a workshop held at the Reinhardswaldschule, Kassel, Germany, July, 1970. Paris: Organisation for Economic Co-operation and Development, 1972.

CHOAT, E. "Introducing the 'Integrated Day' in Junior School". *Forum for the Discussion of New Trends in Education*, 13 (1971), pp. 89-90.

Choat, E. "Curriculum design in the primary school". *Forum for the Discussion of New Trends in Education*, 17 (1974), pp. 15-17.

Connelly, D. "On the integration of school learning". *Education Canada*, 12 (1972), pp. 23-27.

Cropley, A.J. "Some psychological reflections on lifelong education". In Dave, R.H. (ed.). *Foundations of Lifelong Education*. Oxford: Pergamon Press; Unesco Institute for Education, 1976. (Advances in Lifelong Education 1).

Cropley, A.J. *Lifelong Education: A Psychological Analysis*. Oxford: Pergamon Press; Unesco Institute for Education, 1977. (Advances in Lifelong Education 3).

Dave, R.H. *Lifelong Education and School Curriculum*. Hamburg: Unesco Institute for Education, 1973. (uie monographs 1).

Dave, R.H. (ed.). *Foundations of Lifelong Education*. Oxford: Pergamon Press; Unesco Institute for Education, 1976. (Advances in Lifelong Education 1).

Dineen, F.P. "Linguistics and the social sciences". In Sherif, M. and Sherif, C.E. (eds.). *Interdisciplinary Relationships in the Social Sciences*. Chicago: Aldine, 1969.

Doyal, L. "Interdisciplinary studies in higher education". *Universities Quarterly*, 28 (1974), pp. 470-487.

Dressel. "The meaning and significance of integration". In Henry, N.B. (ed.). *The Integration of Educational Experiences*. The Fifty-Seventh Yearbook of the National Society for the Study of Education, Part III. Chicago, Illinois: University of Chicago Press, 1958.

Dunlop, O.J. *Modern Studies: Origins, Aims and Development*. London: MacMillan, 1977.

Dyasi, H.M. "Technology and general education: integrated science education in African primary schools". *Prospects: Quarterly Review of Education*, IV (1974), pp. 63-71.

Eisner, E.W. "Instructional and expressive educational objectives: their formulation and use in curriculum". In Popham, W.J.; Eisner, E.W.; Sullivan, H.J. and Tyler, L.L. *Instructional Objectives*. Chicago: Rand McNally, 1969. (American Educational Research Association Monograph Series on Curriculum Evaluation No.3).

Esland, G.M. "Teaching and learning as the organisation of knowledge". In Young, M.F.D. *Knowledge and Control*. London: Collier-Macmillan, 1971.

Fisher, R.J. *Learning How to Learn: The English Primary School and Primary Education*. New York: Harcourt Brace Jovanovich, 1972.

Gilliat, P. "Integration in years one and two". *General Education*, 23 (1974), pp. 35-39.

Gregson, A. and Quinn, W. "Quiet revolution". *Dialogue*, 10 (1972), pp. 6-7.

Gwynn, J.M. and Chase, J.B. *Curriculum Principles and Social Trends*. New York: MacMillan, 1969.

Haigh, G. *'Integrate'*. London: Allen and Unwin, 1975.

Hall, W.C. "Aims and objectives of integrated science teaching". Schools Council Integrated Science Project. In Richmond, P. E. (ed.). *New Trends in Integrated Science Teaching*. Vol.II. Paris: Unesco, 1973.

Hamilton, D. "The integration of knowledge; practice and problems". *Journal of Curriculum Studies*, 5 (1973), pp.146-155.

Hamilton, D. "Handling innovation in the classroom: two Scottish examples". In Reid, W.A. and Walker, D.F. (eds.). *Case Studies in Curriculum Change Great Britain and the United States*. London and Boston: Routledge and Kegan Paul, 1975.

Heater, D. "The social sciences and history: a model for integration". *General Education*, 18 (1972), pp. 25-28.

Hinds, T.M. "An integrated studies resource area". *Ideas*, 27 (1974), pp. 40-42.

Hirst, P.H. "The logic of the curriculum". *Journal of Curriculum Studies*, 1 (1969), pp. 142-158.

Hirst, P.H. *Knowledge and the Curriculum*. London: Routledge and Kegan Paul, 1974.

Hirst, P.H. and Peters, R.S. *The Logic of Education*. London: Routledge and Kegan Paul, 1970.

Holt, J. *How Children Fail*. London: Pitman, 1964.

Hopkin, A.G. "General studies in the academic secondary school". *Teacher Education in New Countries*, 12 (1971), pp. 24-31.

Hubbard, D.N. and Salt, J. (eds.). *Integrated Studies in the Primary School*. Sheffield, England: University of Sheffield, Institute of Education, 1970.

Hudson, L. *Contrary Imaginations*. A Psychological Study of the English Schoolboy. Harmondsworth: Penguin, 1967.

Hudson, L. *Frames of Mind*. Harmondsworth: Penguin, 1970.

James, C. *Young Lives at Stake*. A Reappraisal of Secondary Schools. London: Collins, 1968.

James, C. "The open curriculum". *University of London, Institute of Education Bulletin*, 19 (Autumn, 1969), pp. 12-15.

Jeffreys, M.V.C. *Personal Values in the Modern World*. Harmondsworth: Penguin, 1962.

Jenkins, D. and Shipman, M.D. *Curriculum: An Introduction*. London: Open Books, 1976.

Jones, T.D.M. "Straitjacket of integration". *Scottish Educational Journal*, 58 (1975), pp. 475-476.

Kirk, G. "A critique of some arguments in the case for integrated studies". *Scottish Educational Studies*, 5 (1973), pp. 95-102.

Klein, G.S. *Perception, Motives, and Personality*. New York: Knopf, 1970.

Knox, H.M. *Introduction to Educational Method*. London: Oldbourne, 1961.

Kooi, S.W. *Evaluation of Integrated Science Teaching in Malaysia*. Symposium on "Evaluation of Integrated Science Education", Oxford, 26-30 December, 1975. Paris: Unesco, 1975. (mimeo.)

Krasilchik, M. *Evaluation of Teaching of Integrated Science in Brazil*. Symposium on "Evaluation of Integrated Science Education", Oxford, 26-30 December, 1975. Paris: Unesco, 1975. (mimeo.)

Kratwohl, D.R.; Bloom, B.S. and Masia, B.B. *Taxonomy of Educational Objectives: Handbook II: Affective Domain*. New York: Longmans Green, 1964.

Lamb, A.; Carroll, J.; Bone, R. and Moules, B. "The development of IDE in a secondary modern school". *Ideas*, 26 (1973), pp. 50-53.

Lamm, Z. "Teaching and curriculum planning". *Journal of Curriculum Studies*, 1 (1969), pp. 159-171.

Lancashire, A. "Integrated studies - a theological approach". *Learning for Living*, 12 (1973), pp. 8-11.

Lawton, D. "The idea of an integrated curriculum". *University of London, Institute of Education Bulletin*, 19 (1969), pp. 5-11.

Lawton, D. *Class, Culture and the Curriculum.* London: Routledge and Kegan Paul, 1975.

Lee, D.M. "Educational psychology and the integrated curriculum". In Unesco. *On an Integrated Approach to the Primary Curriculum.* Paris: Unesco, 1971. (mimeo.)

Lengrand, P. *An Introduction to Lifelong Education.* Paris: Unesco, 1970.

Levit, M. "Interdisciplinary education and understanding the disciplines". In Levit, M. (ed.). *Curriculum.* Urbana, Illinois: University of Illinois Press, 1971.

Luke, H. "English in integrated studies". *English in Education*, 5 (1971), pp. 30-36.

Lynch, J. *Reformkonzeptionen der Lehrerbildung in Grossbritannien.* Weinheim: Beltz, 1977.

Macmurray, J. *The Structure of Religious Experience.* London: Faber and Faber, 1936.

Markham, K.A. "Accountancy and the curriculum: or how to achieve a philosophical balance". *Education and Social Science*, 1 (1970), pp. 141-144.

Mayer, V.J. and Richmond, J.M. *Evaluation Instruments for Integrated Science Teaching.* Symposium on "Evaluation of Integrated Science Education", Oxford, 26-30 December, 1975. Paris: Unesco, 1975. (mimeo.)

Meister, R.W. "What about 'unified arts' in the middle school?" *Educational Leadership.* 31 (1973), pp. 233-235.

Milton, O. *Alternatives to the Traditional.* San Francisco: Jossey-Bass, 1973.

Mitchell, P.; Hogan, D. and West, D. "Integration and innovation: a trilogy". *General Education*, 18 (1972), pp. 33-46.

Moore, R.F. "History and integrated studies: surrender or survival?" *Teaching History*, 4 (1975), pp. 109-112.

Morris, J.W. "Towards a balanced curriculum". *Trends in Education*, 18 (1970), pp. 10-17.

Moulez, G.J. *Psychology for Effective Teaching*. New York: Holt, Rhinehart and Winston, 1973.

Musgrove, F. "A widening gap between students of science and arts". *Educational Research*, 13 (1971), pp. 113-118.

Musgrove, F. "Power and the integrated curriculum". *Journal of Curriculum Studies*. 5 (1973), pp. 3-12.

Neagley, R.L. and Evans, N.D. *Handbook for Effective Curriculum Development*. Englewood Cliffs, New Jersey: Prentice-Hall, 1967.

New Zealand Post Primary Teachers' Association. *Education in Change*. Harlow: Longman, 1971.

Nicholls, R. "Dilemmas at 14 Plus". *Trends in Education*. 29 (1973), pp- 33-37.

Nisbet, S. *Purpose in the Curriculum*. London: University of London Press, 1957.

O.E.C.D. (Organisation for Economic Cooperation and Development). *Modernizing our Schools: Curriculum Improvement and Educational Development*. Paris: O.E.C.D., 1966.

Oeser, O.A. *Teacher, Pupil and Task*. London: Tavistock, 1960.

Oliver, A.I. *Curriculum Improvement*. A Guide to Problems, Principles, and Procedures. New York: Dodd, Mead and Company, 1968.

Owen, J.G. *The Management of Curriculum Development*. Cambridge, England: Cambridge University Press, 1973.

Owens, G. "Integrated studies". *General Education*, 18 (1972), pp. 19-24.

Phenix, P.H. *Realms of Meaning*. New York: McGraw-Hill, 1964.

Pilley, J.G. "The boundaries of subjects". *Researches and Studies*, 20 (1959), pp. 69-74.

Pring, R. "Curriculum integration". In Hooper, R. (ed.). *The Curriculum; Context, Design and Development*. Edinburgh: Oliver and Boyd/Open University Press, 1971.

Richmond, W.K. *The School Curriculum*. London: Metheun, 1971.

Rogers, C.R. "Towards a science of the person". In Wann, T.W. (ed.). *Behaviourism and Phenomenology*. Chicago, Illinois: University of Chicago Press, 1964.

Ross, A.M.; Razzell, A.G. and Badcock, E.H. *The Curriculum in the Middle Years*. Schools Council Working Paper 55. London: Evans/Methuen, 1975.

Salt, J. "Problems of integrated education". *Trends in Education*. 16 (1969), pp. 23-27.

Schools Council Integrated Studies. *Exploration Man: An Introduction to Integrated Studies*. London: Schools Council/ Oxford University Press, 1972.

Schwab, J.J. "Structures and dynamics of knowledge". In Levit, M. (ed.). *Curriculum*. Urbana, Illinois: University of Illinois Press, 1971.

Scottish Education Department Consultative Committee on the Curriculum. *The Structure of the Curriculum in the Third and Fourth Years of the Secondary School*. London: H.M.S.O., 1977.

Scribner, S. and Cole, M. "Cognitive consequences of formal and informal education". *Science*, 182 (1973), pp. 553-559.

Sellick, D. "Integration without fears". *Spectrum*, 7 (1975), pp. 13-15.

Shaver, J.P. and Larkins, A.G. "Research on teaching social studies". In Travers, R.M.W. (ed.). *Second Handbook of Research on Teaching*. Chicago: Rand McNally, 1973.

Shimbori, M. "Lifelong integrated education". In Dave, R.H. (ed.). *Reflections on Lifelong Education and the School*. Hamburg: Unesco Institute for Education, 1975. (uie monographs 3).

Shipman, M. "Curriculum for inequality". In Hooper, R. (ed.). *The Curriculum: Context, Design and Development*. Edinburgh: Oliver and Boyd/Open University Press, 1971.

Simpson, E.J. "The classification of educational objectives". *Illinois Teacher of Home Economics*. X (1966-67), pp. 116-144.

Simpson, R.H. *Teacher Self-Evaluation*. New York: MacMillan, 1966.

Skilbeck, M. "Forms of curriculum integration". *General Education*, 18 (1972), pp. 7-13.

Snow, C.P. *The Two Cultures and the Scientific Revolution*. Cambridge, England: Cambridge University Press, 1959.

Stenhouse, L. "The humanities curriculum project". *Journal of Curriculum Studies*, I (1968), pp. 26-30.

Stenhouse, L. "Some limitations of the use of objectives in curriculum research and planning". *Paedagogica Europaea*, 6 (1970), pp. 73-83.

Suchodolski, B. "Lifelong education - some philosophical aspects". In Dave, R.H. (ed.). *Foundations of Lifelong Education*. Oxford: Pergamon Press; Unesco Institute for Education, 1976. (Advances in Lifelong Education 1).

Sutton, C. *What Skills Are Needed to Teach Integrated Science and How Can their Development be Monitored?* Symposium on "Evaluation of Integrated Science Education", Oxford, 26-30 December, 1975. Paris: Unesco, 1975. (mimeo.)

Taba, H. *Curriculum Development: Theory and Practice*. New York: Harcourt, Brace and World, 1962.

Tawney, D.A. *What Evaluation Might Do for Curriculum Development in Integrated Sciences*. Symposium on "Evaluation of Integrated Science Education", Oxford, 26-30 December, 1975. Paris: Unesco, 1975. (mimeo.)

Taylor, J. *Organising and Integrating the Infant Day*. London: Allen & Unwin, 1971.

Team of Staff from Llanedeyrn High School. Cardiff, Wales. "A foundation year". *Forum for the Discussion of New Trends in Education*, 14 (1972), pp. 76-78.

Trump, J.L. and Baynham, D. *Focus on Change - Guide to Better Schools*. Chicago: Rand McNally, 1961.

Tykociner, J.T. "Zetetics and areas of knowledge". In Elam, S. (ed.). *Education and the Structure of Knowledge*. Chicago: Rand McNally, 1964.

Tyler, R.W. *Basic Principles of Curriculum and Instruction*. Chicago: University of Chicago Press, 1949.

Tyler, R.W. "Curriculum organisation". In Henry, N.B. (ed.). *The Integration of Educational Experiences*. The Fifty-Seventh Yearbook of the National Society for the Study of Education, Part III. Chicago: University of Chicago Press, 1958.

Unesco. *Meeting of Experts on Curriculum of General Education*. Final Report. Moscow, USSR, 16-23 January, 1968. Paris: Unesco, 1968. (mimeo.)

Unesco. *Meeting of Experts on the Place and Function of Aesthetic Education in General Education*. Final Report. Paris, Unesco House, 2-7 December, 1974. Paris: Unesco, 1975a. (mimeo.)

Unesco. *Meeting of Experts on Secondary Education and the World of Work.* Final Report. Copenhagen, 9-14 December, 1974. Paris: Unesco, 1975b. (mimeo.)

Unesco. *Lifelong Education: The Curriculum and Basic Learning Needs.* Final Report of Regional Seminar, Chiangmai, Thailand, 7-15 June, 1976. Bangkok: Unesco, 1976a.

Unesco. *Curriculum Development for Work-Oriented Education.* Report of a Regional Field Operational Seminar, Tokyo, 19 September - 17 October, 1975. Bangkok: Unesco, 1976b. (mimeo.)

Unesco. *Meeting of Experts on the Content of Education in the Context of Lifelong Education.* Final Report. Paris, Unesco House, 20-25 October, 1975. Paris: Unesco, 1976c. (mimeo.)

Vaideanu, G. "Le contenu de l'enseignement dans le contexte de l'éducation permanente". *Bulletin du Greti. Techniques d'Instruction*, 4 (1976), pp. 11-17.

Walton, J. *The Integrated Day in Theory and Practice.* London: Ward Lock, 1971.

Warwick, D. *Curriculum Structure and Design.* London: University of London Press, 1975.

Whitehead, A.N. *The Aims of Education.* London: Williams & Norgate, 1932.

Whitfield, R. (ed.). *Disciplines of the Curriculum.* New York: McGraw-Hill, 1971.

Williams, A. "Integrated studies project". *Forum*, 16 (1973), pp. 12-14.

Winthrop, H. "Specialisation and intellectual integration in liberal education". *Educational Theory*, 17 (1967), pp.25-31.

Wise, G. "Integrative education for a disintegrated world". *Teachers' College Record*, 67 (1966), pp. 391-401.

Wolsk, D. *An Experience-Centred Curriculum.* Exercises in Perception, Communication and Action. Paris: Unesco, 1975.

Young, M.F.D. *Knowledge and Control.* London: Collier-MacMillan, 1971.

Zverev, I.D. "Interdisciplinarity in school education in the U.S.S.R.". *Prospects: Quarterly Review of Education*, 5 (1975), pp. 445-455.

INDEX